natural cakes

natural cakes

Contents

Introduction

Today more than ever we are aware of the importance of a healthy and balanced diet. We recognize more and more the need to cook at home, starting from raw materials, and realize that what we eat has a significant impact on our body, our psyche, and our general well-being. We are increasingly aware of the advantage of eating well and the importance of unrefined, whole, and natural ingredients.

NATURAL BAKING

Every day more and more versatile ingredients and new cooking methods that involve an abundance of vegetables, pulses, and whole foods are available and I am so pleased to see that this culinary revolution has finally started to focus also on desserts. The purpose of this book is to celebrate the choice of a natural and healthy diet even for the sweetest things in life, cakes. The starting point is the use of unrefined, whole-grain, organic, seasonal and, whenever possible, locally sourced ingredients. The recipes in this book are not sugar-free, because they contain fruits, vegetables, and other types of sweeteners, but the cakes in this book are all naturally sweetened with ingredients such as apple purée and mashed banana or unrefined sugar such as coconut sugar.

EASY SWAPPING FOR REFINED INGREDIENTS

Obviously baking without the "traditional" ingredients like superfine sugar or all-purpose flour can seem intimidating, but in the end it is not as difficult as it seems. In most cases you will end up using the same ingredients that you would normally use in a "classic" recipe, but with the help and the addition of some special ingredients, most of which are now available in supermarkets and organic stores. I will show you all the different alternatives available for baking cakes. The idea is to have a number of recipes available that can be used both by people who have decided to start eating more naturally with simple ingredients rich in nutritional principles and low in sugar, but also by those suffering from intolerances and allergies.

HOW TO USE THIS BOOK

Some people have an unpleasant and sometimes dangerous physical reaction called "food hypersensitivity" when they eat certain foods that can involve the immune system—this is called "food allergy." When it doesn't involve the immune system it is called "food intolerance." It is estimated that more than 20% of the populations of most developed countries suffer from food allergies and whatever the causes are, it is something that is now part of our experience. Each chapter of the book is dedicated to one of the main ingredients used when baking cakes—dairy, sugar, flour, and egg—and offers alternative ingredients to make natural cakes. At the beginning of each chapter I will explain the function of the ingredient, the different alternatives, and how to use them. Obviously the transition from the consumption of refined high sugars to more natural alternatives is a process that requires adjustment, but after a few weeks your sensitivity to flavors will have increased and you will appreciate and recognize the natural aromas and flavors more. Natural sweeteners also have additional cooking properties; for example, dates are very aromatic and maple syrup or apple purée will add moisture to baked goods.

BAKING BASICS

- Make sure you read through the recipe as this will make you understand what equipment you need and if you have all the ingredients.
- Get organized by laying out all the ingredients, measuring them with a digital scale and measuring spoons, and don't forget to take note of any changes you are making.
- Preheating the oven ensures that the batter reaches the desired temperature to achieve the necessary physical changes during cooking. The temperature and cooking times may vary from oven to oven, so keep an eye on the cake the first time you are baking it to see if you need to change something.

- Use the correct cake pan size stated in the recipe as this will ensure the batter fits in the pan and bakes according to the recipe.
- Always measure coconut oil in its liquid form.
- Always cream the butter and the sugar until light and fluffy before proceeding to the next step.
- Prepare your pan properly following the instructions on page 14. Let cakes cool completely on a wire rack before icing.

Ingredients to use

Source your food locally and buy seasonally as much as possible.
Considering the large amount of pesticides used in farming,
try to use organic products as this will also help the environment.

SUGAR ALTERNATIVES

- Coconut sugar
- Maple syrup
- Honey
- Apple purée
- Mashed banana
- Date paste

DAIRY ALTERNATIVES

- Cashew milk
- Almond milk
- Coconut milk
- Oat milk
- Rice milk
- Quinoa milk
- Nut butter
- Coconut butter
- Coconut oil
- Vegetable oil
- Coconut yogurt

FLOUR ALTERNATIVES

- Quinoa flour
- Millet flour
- Oat flour
- Sorghum flour
- White rice flour
- Almond flour
- Brown rice flour
- Buckwheat flour
- Coconut flour
- Teff flour
- Polenta

EGG ALTERNATIVES

- Apple purée
- Mashed banana
- Flaxseed
- Chia seed
- Arrowroot powder
- Potato flour
- Baking soda
- Vinegar
- Vegetarian gelatin

BUYING AND STORING TIPS

- Buy seasonal ingredients and freeze them to hold their flavor and help them last longer. Label your frozen items clearly so you can reuse easily.
- Use mason jars, empty jam jars, bottles, and glass containers in all shapes to store your ingredients.
- Store all dry ingredients in airtight containers and in a cool, dry, dark place, off the floor and away from materials with strong odors like soap, chemicals, or onions and take a note, if needed, of the expiration date. Keep liquids in their own bottles.
- Keep spices, vanilla beans, and liquids in a cool, dry place away from any direct heat sources.
- Buy grains, natural sweeteners, nuts, seeds, and dried fruits in bulk.

Sweet flavor boosters

Baking can be improved and enhanced with the selection and addition of seasonal fruit and vegetables, spices, and nuts that, together with the main ingredients, will add fabulous flavors and nutrients to your cakes, without the use of refined sugars.

NUTS
Super nutritional and contain tons of protein and good fat.

SPICES
A well-stocked spice cabinet should contain cinnamon and cardamom.

VANILLA
I only use unsweetened vanilla extract and vanilla beans for a warm aroma.

CACAO
Contains antioxidants, iron, calcium, and magnesium.

CITRUS
Citrus zest is packed with oils and is full of aroma and flavor.

BEET
Great source of fiber, iron, vitamin B9, manganese, potassium, and vitamin C.

AVOCADO
A rich source of heart-healthy monounsaturated fat and many vitamins.

FLOWER WATERS
Start by adding a few drops at a time to liquid ingredients.

Natural colorings

Natural powders are produced from frozen dried berries or vegetables that are ground without any other additives, but they tend to be less vivid than artificial color additives. They are much healthier than chemically manufactured food colorings.

RED

Beet powder: a teaspoon at a time as you will also add flavor to the cake.

PINK

Pure raspberry juice: you may need to reduce the liquid in the recipe.

ORANGE

Paprika: a teaspoon at a time as you will also add flavor to the cake.

GREEN

Matcha (green tea) powder: rich in antioxidants and fiber.

PURPLE

Grape juice: you may need to reduce the liquid in the recipe.

YELLOW

Turmeric: a teaspoon at a time as you will also add flavor to the cake.

BROWN

Cinnamon: a teaspoon at a time as you will also add flavor to the cake.

BLACK

Activated charcoal powder: has no flavor; makes a dark slate color.

Useful equipment

Before you begin baking, ensure you have all the tools and equipment that you'll need on hand. Here is a summary of the some of the recommended items needed for baking all manner of cakes.

1. MEASURING CUP AND MIXING BOWLS
Glass, metal, or ceramic.

2. MICROPLANE ZESTER
For finely grating citrus fruits or to grate chocolate to create chocolate shavings.

3. WHISKS
A small hand whisk and a larger balloon whisk are good to have on hand.

4. MEASURING EQUIPMENT
Measuring spoons and digital scales should always be used for maximum accuracy.

5. PEELER
For peeling the skin from fruit and for making chocolate shavings.

6. SPATULAS, KITCHEN KNIFE, AND SCISSORS
For endless uses in the kitchen.

7. PARCHMENT PAPER
To line trays and cake pans.

8. WIRE RACK
To cool cakes after baking.

9. CAKE PANS
A selection of round, Bundt, and mini Bundt cake pans; cupcake, loaf, and springform pans; and mini-cake silicone molds.

10. SIEVE
To sift and eliminate parts of an ingredient or separate clumps from all dry ingredients.

11. CUPCAKE LINERS
A convenient and easy way to line cupcake and muffin pans.

OTHER USEFUL ITEMS:
Nut milk bag—To filter the nut milks.

Blender—For grinding nuts, creamy fillings, and tough sticky ingredients like dates.

Freestanding or handheld electric mixer—This will take all the effort out of beating cake batters and mixing icing ingredients.

HOW TO LINE A ROUND CAKE PAN

Preparing the cake pan properly takes a matter of moments and is one little job that is worth the effort; it simply involves us getting creative with our scissors.

Lines: 1 round cake pan
PREP TIME: 10 min.

any size round cake pan
sheet of parchment paper larger than the pan

01 Place a round cake pan on top of a sheet of parchment paper and draw a circle around it. Cut out with scissors.

02 Cut a strip of parchment paper long enough to cover the pan's circumference and the height, plus an added ½ inch (1 cm) overhang. Fold over the overhang along the long edge.

03 Use scissors to snip diagonal cuts at 1 inch (2.5 cm) intervals along the folded part of the paper strip. Lightly grease the inside of the pan.

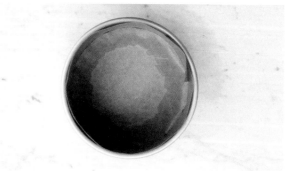

04 Line the inside of the pan, placing the paper strip around the edge with the snipped part sitting on the base of the pan. Place the cut-out circle in the pan last.

HOW TO LINE A LOAF CAKE PAN

Lining a loaf pan with parchment paper is one of the easiest ways to save time and energy when making a cake. All you have to do is lift the edges of the paper to pull your treat out of the pan once baked.

Lines: 1 loaf cake pan
PREP TIME:
10 min.

any size loaf pan
sheet of parchment paper larger than the pan

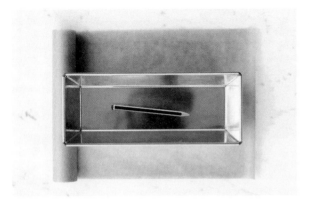

01 Place a loaf cake pan on top of a sheet of parchment paper and fold the paper up on the left, right, front, and back sides of the pan.

02 With a pencil, draw the bottom of the pan on the paper and crease the paper along the shape of the loaf pan.

03 Make large diagonal cuts in each corner of the paper and cut out one triangle. Repeat this process on all corners. Place the paper in the pan and fold in the corners.

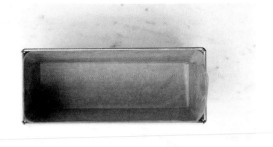

04 Once it fits well, remove the paper, grease the inside of the pan and then replace the paper. This method ensures that there are no gaps in the lining.

SUGAR ALTERNATIVES

Sugar in baking

Sugar adds sweetness and flavor, creates softness and finesse in consistency, colors the crust, increases the durability of the cake by retaining moisture inside, provides food for the yeast, and acts as a leavening agent with the help of fats and eggs.

Natural sweeteners

There are different types of alternative sugars that are not very refined and therefore very close to their natural form and still contain some nutrients, such as vitamins, minerals, and fiber.

Apple purée
Nutrition per 3½ oz. (100 g)

95 calories

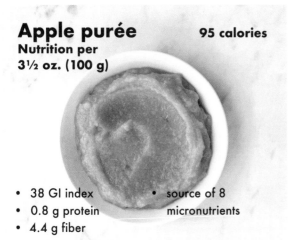

- 38 GI index
- 0.8 g protein
- 4.4 g fiber
- source of 8 micronutrients

Honey
Nutrition per 3½ oz. (100 g)

304 calories

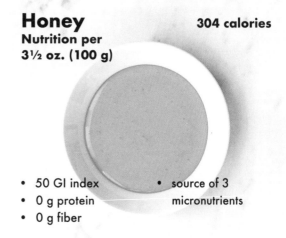

- 50 GI index
- 0 g protein
- 0 g fiber
- source of 3 micronutrients

Coconut sugar
Nutrition per 3½ oz. (100 g)

375 calories

- 30 GI index
- 0 g protein
- 0 g fiber
- source of 6 micronutrients

Maple syrup
Nutrition per 3½ oz. (100 g)

260 calories

- 54 GI index
- 0 g protein
- 0 g fiber
- source of 5 micronutrients

Date paste
(see page 20)
Nutrition per 3½ oz. (100 g)

285 calories

- 55 GI index
- 1.81 g protein
- 6.7 g fiber
- source of 10 micronutrients

Mashed banana
Nutrition per 3½ oz. (100 g)

105 calories

- 10 GI index
- 1.3 g protein
- 3.5 g fiber
- source of 4 micronutrients

How to replace refined

apple purée

| ½ cup (100 g) sugar | = | 3½ oz. (100 g) unsweetened apple purée | You can use fresh or dried fruits instead of superfine sugar in cake recipes. By doing this you will not only add the natural flavor of the fruit itself, but also the vitamins, minerals, fiber, and phytonutrients that the fruit contains. Apple purée lightens the caloric density of baked goods while adding fiber. The finished cake will have a tender, crumbly texture and a sweeter flavor. |

coconut sugar

| ½ cup (100 g) sugar | = | ½ cup (100 g) coconut sugar | Made from the sap of the coconut palm that has been extracted, boiled, and dehydrated. It has a deep, nutty, warm caramel flavor and doesn't taste like coconut. Always buy organic when possible. It is a natural sugar that contains small amounts of nutrients including fiber, iron, zinc, magnesium, calcium, potassium, and antioxidants. |

date paste

| ½ cup (100 g) sugar | = | ½ recipe Date Paste (see page 20) | Made from fresh dates, date paste is an all-natural and nutritionally dense sweetener that increases the health benefits in your baked goods. Dates are known for helping to relieve constipation, most likely due to their soluble fiber and magnesium content, and are a plant-based source of iron and vitamin C. |

sugar in baking

honey

½ cup (100 g) sugar   **=**   5 tablespoons (75 ml) honey

Honey is made by bees out of nectar gathered from flowers to feed the hive. It comes in a wide range of different versions, greatly depending on the flowers the bees have been feeding from. Try to buy local where possible and be careful as cheap honey may be blended with glucose to reduce production costs.

maple syrup

½ cup (100 g) sugar   **=**   5 tablespoons (75 ml) maple syrup

Made by boiling down the sap from Canadian maple trees until the sugars condense into thick syrup. It has a deep, caramel flavor and comes in different grades. Try to avoid the "maple flavored syrup" as it isn't real maple syrup. Natural maple syrup contains minerals, such as calcium and potassium, iron, zinc, and manganese, and at least 24 different antioxidants.

mashed banana

½ cup (100 g) sugar   **=**   3 tablespoons (50 g) mashed banana

Puréed banana is a nutritional powerhouse, packed with energy-giving carbohydrates and loaded with valuable micronutrients. Rich in moisture, it can create a moist and tender cake. Bananas will add more moisture to the cake recipe, so you might need to adjust the other ingredients accordingly.

HOW TO MAKE DATE PASTE

Dates are a powerhouse sweetener. They contain minerals like selenium, magnesium, manganese, and copper, which are thought to keep bones healthy and help to prevent osteoporosis.

Makes: 1 lb. (450 g)

PREP TIME: 10 min., plus 4 hours soaking

1 lb. (450 g) Medjool dates, pitted
½ cup (120 ml) water

01 Soak the dates for 4 hours in a jar with the water.

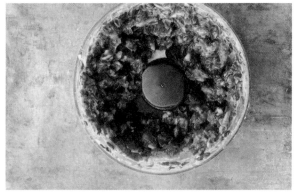

02 Transfer the dates and soaking water to a food processor or blender and process for 4 minutes.

03 Scrape down the bowl to make sure all the dates are incorporated and process for another 4 minutes until smooth and creamy.

04 Transfer to a mason jar and keep it in the fridge for up to 3 months.

HOW TO USE A VANILLA BEAN

dairy-, gluten-, and egg-free

You can also make a simple paste by adding 1 teaspoon hot water to the vanilla seeds and stirring until a light paste forms. One vanilla bean is the equivalent of 1 tablespoon vanilla extract.

Makes: 5 g

PREP TIME: 1 min.

1 vanilla bean

01 Place the vanilla bean on a cutting board and place the tip of the knife flat down along the length.

02 Slowly cut into the pod, trying to only slice through the top and not punching through the bottom. Pull the pod open.

03 Using the side of the knife, scrape the vanilla seeds from the pod, working one half at a time.

04 The seeds can be mixed straight into your recipe along with the other ingredients.

10 min. / 30 min.

The subtle sweet caramel flavor from the coconut sugar combined with the super nutrition of the quinoa makes this a perfect cake to have with tea.

Chocolate mud cake

Serves: 10–12

7 tablespoons (100 g) unsalted butter, plus extra for greasing

5 oz. (150 g) dark chocolate

4 eggs, lightly beaten

1 tablespoon coffee

1 teaspoon vanilla extract

¼ cup (60 g) plain yogurt

⅓ cup (80 ml) coconut milk

½ cup (60 g) quinoa flour

1 cup (100 g) spelt flour

3 tablespoons (30 g) rice flour

3 tablespoons (20 g) raw cacao powder

½ cup (100 g) coconut sugar

2½ teaspoons baking powder

½ teaspoon salt

Preheat the oven to 325°F (160°C). Grease and line a 9-inch (23 cm) cake pan with parchment paper. Melt the butter and chocolate in a heatproof bowl set over a pan of simmering water (making sure the bottom of the bowl doesn't touch the water). Add the eggs, coffee, vanilla, yogurt, and coconut milk and stir to combine. Sift together all the dry ingredients in a bowl and then fold in the chocolate mixture.

Pour into the pan and bake for 30 minutes or until cooked and a skewer inserted in the center comes out clean. Leave to cool in the pan completely before serving.

Cake will keep for 2–4 days in the refrigerator, stored in an airtight container. Allow to come up to room temperature before serving.

20 min. / 35 min.

Rich, dark, and full of nutty, complex flavors from the spelt flour, this cake has a classic cream cheese frosting, but you could swap it for Cashew Nut Frosting (see page 202) if preferred.

Carrot cake

Serves: 10

1 cup (250 ml) vegetable oil, plus extra for greasing
4 large eggs
½ cup (100 g) coconut sugar
2 cups (200 g) peeled and coarsely grated carrots
1½ cups (150 g) spelt flour
1½ cups (150 g) almond flour
2 teaspoons baking powder
1 teaspoon pumpkin pie spice
1 teaspoon ground ginger
⅔ cup (75 g) walnuts, roughly chopped, to decorate

Frosting

3½ tablespoons (50 g) butter, at room temperature
1 tablespoon (25 g) acacia honey
9 oz. (250 g) full-fat cream cheese
1 teaspoon vanilla extract
Grated zest and juice of 1 orange

Preheat the oven to 350°F (180°C). Grease and line an 8-inch (20 cm) round cake pan with parchment paper. Whisk the oil, eggs, and sugar in a large mixing bowl until well combined. Gently fold in the carrots and all other ingredients, except the walnuts, and mix until evenly blended.

Pour the batter into the pan and bake for 35 minutes or until the cake has risen. Leave to cool in the pan for 5 minutes and then turn out onto a wire rack to cool completely.

Meanwhile, place all the ingredients for the frosting in a bowl and whisk until smooth. Spread the frosting evenly over the top of the cake and decorate with the chopped walnuts.

This cake will keep in the fridge, un-iced, for 3 days.

10 min. / 15 min.

A classic cake recipe that features layers of light sponge sandwiched together with velvety cream and juicy strawberries.

Victoria sponge cake with fresh strawberries

Serves: 8

¾ cup (175 g) butter, plus extra for greasing
½ cup (100 g) coconut sugar
Seeds from 1 vanilla bean (see page 21)
3 eggs, lightly beaten
½ cup (80 g) rice flour
⅓ cup (45 g) cornstarch
⅓ cup (45 g) arrowroot
2 teaspoons baking powder
1 tablespoon powdered sugar, for dusting

Filling

1 cup (250 ml) whipping cream
1 tablespoon powdered sugar
1½ cups (250 g) strawberries, hulled and quartered

Preheat the oven to 350°F (180°C). Grease and line two 7-inch (18 cm) round cake pans with parchment paper. Place all the ingredients, except the powdered sugar, in a bowl and whisk until well blended. Divide the batter evenly between the pans and bake for 15 minutes or until a skewer inserted in the middle comes out clean. Leave to cool in the pans for 5 minutes before turning out onto a wire rack to cool completely.

Whisk the cream and sugar to soft peaks. Sandwich the cakes together with a layer of cream and strawberries and then dust with powdered sugar to finish.

Cake will keep for 1–2 days in the refrigerator, stored in an airtight container. Allow to come up to room temperature before serving.

15 min. / 50 min.

The ground pistachios give this cake a lovely green shade and a wonderful moist texture, lifted by the sharp citrus sweetness of the lemon juice and zest.

Lemon, pistachio, and honey loaf cake

Serves: 8–10

5 tablespoons (75 ml) sunflower oil, plus extra for greasing

1 cup (160 g) rice flour

2 teaspoons baking powder

½ teaspoon salt

3 eggs, separated

7 tablespoons (150 g) honey

Zest and juice of 2 lemons

5 tablespoons (75 g) coconut yogurt

Topping

1 tablespoon honey

1 tablespoon chopped pistachios, to decorate

Preheat the oven to 350°F (170°C). Grease and line an 8 by 4-inch (800 ml) loaf pan with parchment paper. Sift the flour, baking powder, and salt together. Whisk the egg whites to stiff peaks and set aside. In a separate bowl, whisk the egg yolks, honey, sunflower oil, and lemon juice and zest together until well combined. Add the yogurt and then the flour in 3 batches, stirring thoroughly. Gently fold in the whisked egg whites until just combined.

Spoon the batter into the pan and bake for 50 minutes or until a skewer inserted in the center comes out clean. Leave to cool in the pan for 10 minutes before turning out onto a wire rack to cool completely. Brush with honey and scatter with chopped pistachios.

Cake will keep for 2–4 days in the refrigerator, stored in an airtight container. Allow to come up to room temperature before serving.

10 min. / 20 min.

A classic recipe baked with healthy root vegetables that ensures a beautifully moist cake and a natural red color.

Red velvet cake

Serves: 10

1 cup plus 1 tablespoon (250 ml) sunflower oil, plus extra for greasing

9 oz. (250 g) fresh beets, finely grated

1½ cups (150 g) spelt flour

⅔ cup (100 g) rice flour

½ cup (50 g) cornstarch

4 teaspoons baking powder

2 teaspoons beet powder

1 tablespoon raw cacao powder

¾ cup (175 ml) milk

⅓ cup (85 g) plain yogurt

¼ cup (60 ml) coffee

2 eggs, lightly beaten

½ cup (100 g) coconut sugar

2 teaspoons vanilla extract

1 teaspoon balsamic vinegar

Frosting

10½ oz. (300 g) cream cheese

2 tablespoons honey

1 tablespoon vanilla extract

1 cup (250 ml) whipping cream

Preheat the oven to 350°F (180°C). Grease and line two 8-inch (20 cm) round pans with parchment paper. Mix the beet, flours, cornstarch, baking powder, beet powder, and cacao powder together. In a mixing bowl, whisk all the other ingredients and then fold in the beet mixture. Divide the batter between the two pans and bake for 20 minutes or until a skewer inserted in the center comes out clean. Leave to cool for 5 minutes in the pans before turning out onto a wire rack to cool.

To make the frosting, whisk the cream cheese with the honey and vanilla. Whip the cream to soft peaks and then gently combine the two mixtures. Spread half the icing on one cake, sit the other cake on top and spread the remaining icing evenly over the top and sides of the cake to finish. Keep in the fridge until ready to serve.

Cake will keep for 1–2 days in the refrigerator, stored in an airtight container. Allow to come up to room temperature before serving.

15 min. / 30 min.

This cake is perfect for any seasonal fruits available—it will be great with apricots, plums, or pineapple that will add a natural sweetness to the cake.

Nectarine upside-down cake

Serves: 10

2½ oz. (75 g) soft dried apricots
½ cup plus 3 tablespoons (150 g) unsalted butter, plus extra for greasing
6 tablespoons (75 g) coconut sugar
⅔ cup (100 g) cornstarch
½ cup (50 g) spelt flour
½ cup (50 g) almond flour
1 teaspoon baking powder
2 teaspoons vanilla extract
3 eggs

Topping

3 tablespoons (35 g) coconut sugar
5 tablespoons (70 g) unsalted butter
4 fresh nectarines, pitted and quartered

Place the dried apricots in a bowl, cover with boiling water, and soak for 15 minutes. Preheat the oven to 350°F (180°C). Grease and line an 8-inch (20 cm) cake pan with parchment paper.

To make the topping, whisk the sugar and butter together until light and creamy. Spread over the base of the pan and then arrange the sliced nectarines on top.

Drain the soaked apricots, transfer to a food processor, and blitz to a smooth paste. Whisk with all the other ingredients until combined. Spoon the batter over the nectarines in the pan and bake for 30 minutes or until a skewer inserted in the center comes out clean. Leave to cool in the pan for 5 minutes before turning out carefully onto a serving plate.

Cake will keep for 1–2 days in the refrigerator, stored in an airtight container. Allow to come up to room temperature before serving.

10 min. / 40 min.

Highly nutritious root vegetables, beets add extra moistness to your cake.

Beet Bundt cake

Serves: 10–12

1 cup plus 1 tablespoon (250 ml) sunflower oil, plus extra for greasing

1 tablespoon raw cacao powder, plus extra for dusting

5 eggs

⅔ cup (150 ml) maple syrup

Seeds from 1 vanilla bean (see page 21)

2 cups (200 g) ground almonds

1¾ cups (175 g) spelt flour

2 tablespoons baking powder

½ teaspoon salt

⅔ cup (150 ml) milk

3½ oz. (100 g) beets, cooked and grated

Cacao Sauce (see page 220)

Preheat the oven to 350°F (180°C). Grease an 8-inch (22 cm) Bundt cake pan with oil and dust with cacao powder. Whisk the eggs, maple syrup, and vanilla seeds in a bowl for 3 minutes and then gradually add the oil. Mix all the dry ingredients together and gradually add them to the egg mixture, alternating with the milk. Fold in the beets and mix until combined.

Pour the batter into the pan and bake for 40 minutes or until a skewer inserted in the center comes out clean. Leave in the pan to cool for 10 minutes and then turn onto a wire rack. Pour the Cacao Sauce over the top before serving.

Cake will keep for 2–4 days in the refrigerator, stored in an airtight container. Allow to come up to room temperature before serving.

10 min. / 30 min.

Serve this cake warm with ice cream for a delicious comforting treat.

Almond cake

Serves: 10–12

Vegetable oil, for greasing

4 eggs, separated, room temperature

¼ cup (50 g) coconut sugar

1 teaspoon vanilla extract

1½ cups (150 g) ground almonds

⅓ cup (50 g) rice flour

⅓ cup (30 g) sliced almonds

1 tablespoon honey

Preheat the oven to 350°F (170°C). Grease and line a 9-inch (23 cm) cake pan with parchment paper. In a mixing bowl, whisk the egg yolks, sugar, and vanilla together until light and fluffy. Fold in the ground almonds and rice flour until incorporated. In another bowl, whisk the egg whites until stiff peaks form (about 2 minutes). Fold the egg whites in 3 batches into the almond batter. Do not overmix.

Transfer the batter to the pan and sprinkle the top with the almonds. Bake for 30 minutes or until the top is firm. Leave the cake to rest in the pan for 15 minutes and then place it on a wire rack. Leave to cool to room temperature and then drizzle with honey before serving.

Cake will keep for 2–4 days in the refrigerator, stored in an airtight container. Allow to come up to room temperature before serving.

10 min. / 45 min.

The slightly bitter taste of the quinoa flour is balanced by the sweetness of the date paste and mashed banana in this scrumptious chocolate cake.

Chocolate and maple banana cake

Serves: 10–12

1 cup plus 2 tablespoons (250 g) unsalted butter, melted, plus extra for greasing
¾ cup (100 g) quinoa flour
⅔ cup (100 g) brown rice flour
⅔ cup (100 g) cornstarch
3 tablespoons (30 g) potato starch
⅔ cup (50 g) cacao powder, sifted
1 teaspoon baking soda
½ cup plus 2 tablespoons (120 g) coconut sugar

3 oz. (80 g) Date Paste
5 tablespoons (80 ml) maple syrup
4 eggs
3 mashed bananas
⅔ cup (150 ml) milk
2 teaspoons vanilla extract

Chocolate ganache

2 cups (240 g) sour cream
1 cup (200 g) dark chocolate, melted

Preheat the oven to 350°F (180°C). Grease and line a 9½-inch (24 cm) round springform pan with parchment paper. Place all the ingredients in a large bowl and whisk until smooth. Pour the batter into the prepared pan and bake for 45 minutes or until a skewer inserted in the center comes out clean. Leave to cool in the pan for 10 minutes before turning out onto a wire rack to cool completely.

Make the ganache by whisking the sour cream and chocolate until smooth and then spread over the top of the cake.

Cake will keep for 2–4 days in the refrigerator, stored in an airtight container. Allow to come up to room temperature before serving.

15 min. / 1 hour

A tasty morning tea treat packed with loads of flavor and naturally sweetened with dates and banana.

Date, banana, and rum loaf cake

Serves: 8–10

⅓ cup (80 ml) coconut oil, plus extra for greasing

2 small bananas— 1 mashed and 1 sliced in half lengthwise

½ recipe Date Paste (see page 20)

3 tablespoons dark rum

2 eggs, separated

⅔ cup (85 g) pecans

⅔ cup (100 g) polenta

⅔ cup (100 g) cornstarch

Seeds from 1 vanilla bean (see page 21)

2 teaspoons baking powder

Preheat the oven to 350°F (180°C). Grease and line an 8 by 4-inch (800 ml) loaf pan with parchment paper.

Combine the mashed banana with the Date Paste, rum, and ½ cup (120 ml) water and whisk until smooth. Mix the egg yolks with the oil, nuts, polenta, cornstarch, vanilla, and baking powder in a bowl. Add the mashed banana mixture and stir until combined. Whisk the egg whites to soft peaks and gently fold into the cake batter.

Spoon into the prepared pan and smooth the surface. Place the sliced banana on top and bake for 1 hour or until cooked. Leave to cool in the pan for 10 minutes before turning out onto a wire rack to cool completely.

Cake will keep for 1–2 days in the refrigerator, stored in an airtight container. Allow to come up to room temperature before serving.

HOW TO ROLL A ROULADE

Roulades, with their contrasting spiral of filling and sponge, make a beautiful dessert and they are really easy to make when you get your rolling right.

Serves: 10

PREP / COOK TIME:
10 min. / 45 min.

One 13½-inch (34 cm) Roulade Sponge (see page 44)

1 recipe Cream Filling (see page 44)
fresh berries, to serve

01 As the cake is removed from the oven, lay parchment paper and a lightly damp clean dish towel over it with a large cutting board over the towel. Carefully invert the cake and remove the baking sheet and paper.

02 Using both hands, and starting from the short end, roll the cake and the towel up. The towel will help set up the roulade in its curled position, preventing cracks when it is unrolled. Leave to cool for 30 minutes.

03 Carefully unroll. Don't worry if there are small cracks. Leave to cool for 15 minutes. Use a spatula to spread the filling over the cake, leaving a gap at the far short edge and outer edges but not at the closer end.

04 Reroll the cake without the towel this time. The filling may squish out of the ends a bit, which is fine. Place the roulade on a serving plate with the seam underneath and finish the cake as the recipe directs.

10 min. / 15 min.

The hazelnut flour adds a distinctive rich buttery taste and moisture to the sponge that goes well with blueberries and figs if you want to change the fruit.

Blackberry roulade

Serves: 10

1 cup (80 g) hazelnut flour

⅓ cup (50 g) cornstarch

½ teaspoon salt

5 eggs, separated

2 teaspoons vanilla extract

½ cup (100 g) coconut sugar

Cream filling

14 oz. (400 g) cream cheese

2 tablespoons maple syrup

1 teaspoon vanilla extract

3 tablespoons (50 ml) whipping cream

1 tablespoon cornstarch

To decorate

3 oz. (80 g) Mixed Berry and Vanilla Jam (see page 208)

2 cups (300 g) blackberries

1 tablespoon flaked coconut

Powdered sugar, for dusting

Preheat the oven to 350°F (180°C). Line a 15 x 10 x ¾-in. (38 x 25 x 2 cm) pan with parchment paper. Sift together the flour, cornstarch, and salt. In a bowl, whisk the egg yolks, vanilla, and sugar until light and fluffy. In another bowl, whisk the egg whites to stiff peaks. Carefully fold the egg white into the yolks and then the flour. Spread the batter over the pan and bake for 15 minutes. Roll the roulade (see page 42).

To make the filling, mix the cream cheese, maple syrup, and vanilla. Whip the cream with the cornstarch to soft peaks, then fold into the cheese. Unroll the sponge, and spread a layer of jam followed by the half the cream and the blackberries (reserving some for decoration). Roll up the sponge and place seam side down on a serving plate. Pipe the remaining cream on top. Decorate with the reserved blackberries, flaked coconut, and powdered sugar. Chill for 30 minutes before serving.

dairy-, gluten-, and egg-free

You will not need an oven for this cake because it simply consists of a no-bake almond-coconut crust with a creamy and smooth blueberry filling.

Blueberry cheesecake

Serves: 10

Crust
1 cup (100 g) ground almonds
⅓ cup (25 g) desiccated coconut
¼ oz. (5 g) popped amaranth
½ teaspoon ground cinnamon
1 tablespoon coconut oil
½ teaspoon salt
6 Medjool dates, pitted

Filling
3½ oz. (100 g) coconut butter
¼ cup (60 ml) coconut oil
9 oz. (250 g) blueberries
8½ oz. (240 g) cashews
Grated zest and juice of 1 lemon
5 tablespoons (80 ml) maple syrup
1 teaspoon vanilla extract
¼ cup (60 ml) almond milk
Blueberry powder, for dusting

Line the base and sides of an 8-inch (20 cm) springform cake pan with parchment paper. Place all the crust ingredients in a food processor and pulse a few times until the mixture comes together. Spoon into the prepared pan and press down to form an even base, then refrigerate.

To make the filling, melt the coconut butter and coconut oil in a heatproof bowl set over a pan of simmering water and set aside. Place all the other ingredients in a food processor, reserving a handful of blueberries and the blueberry powder for decoration, and blend until smooth. Slowly add the melted coconut butter and blend until incorporated.

Pour the mixture over the crust and smooth out the top. Transfer to the freezer for a few hours or refrigerate overnight to set. When set, carefully remove from the pan and place on a serving dish. Dust with blueberry powder and decorate with the reserved blueberries to serve.

15 min. / 15 min.

These little cakes are full of flavor with a dense but chewy crumb.

Blueberry and pistachio mini cakes

Makes: 12

1 cup plus 2 tablespoons (250 g) unsalted butter, softened, plus extra for greasing

⅔ cup (130 g) coconut sugar

4 eggs

⅓ cup (50 g) rice flour

½ cup (60 g) sorghum flour

¼ cup (40 g) potato starch

⅓ cup (40 g) arrowroot

2 teaspoons baking powder

1¾ oz. (50 g) ground pistachios

Grated zest and juice of 1 lemon

¾ cup (150 g) blueberries

1 tablespoon cornstarch

To decorate

2 tablespoons honey

2 tablespoons ground pistachios

Preheat the oven to 350°F (170°C). Grease a 12-cup mini cake silicone mold. In a mixing bowl, whisk the butter and sugar until light and creamy. Slowly add the eggs, whisking well after each addition. Sift the flours, starch, arrowroot, and baking powder together. Add the sifted mixture, pistachios, lemon zest, and juice to the egg mixture. Toss the blueberries with the cornstarch as this will stop them sinking. Fold them gently into the batter.

Pour the cake batter into the mini cake pan and bake for 15 minutes. Turn the mini cakes out onto a wire rack to cool down. Lightly brush with honey and decorate with pistachios.

Cakes will keep for 1–2 days in the refrigerator, stored in an airtight container. Allow to come up to room temperature before serving.

10 min. / 30 min.

This Middle Eastern–inspired cake perfectly balances the rich flavor of rose water and a moist texture from the almonds with whipped coconut cream to create an elegantly light cake.

Coconut and rose water cake

Serves: 8

½ cup plus 3 tablespoons (150 g) butter, melted, plus extra for greasing
2 teaspoons rose water
3 eggs
6 tablespoons (80 g) coconut sugar
⅓ cup (50 g) rice flour
⅓ cup (40 g) buckwheat flour
¼ cup (40 g) potato starch
¼ cup (30 g) tapioca flour
½ cup (50 g) ground almonds
½ cup (45 g) desiccated coconut

Frosting

4 cups Whipped Coconut Cream (see page 196)
1 cup (100 g) toasted sliced almonds

Preheat the oven to 350°F (180°C). Grease and line a 7-inch (18 cm) cake pan with parchment paper. Whisk the rose water, eggs, and sugar together until light and creamy. Fold in the flours, potato starch, tapioca, almonds, coconut, and melted butter. Spoon the batter into the pan and bake for 30 minutes or until a skewer inserted in the center comes out clean. Cool in the pan for 10 minutes and then turn out onto a wire rack.

Spread the Whipped Coconut Cream over the cake. Finish with the sliced almonds to decorate.

Cake will keep for 1–2 days in the refrigerator, stored in an airtight container. Allow to come up to room temperature before serving.

15 min. / 55 min.

This is really a straightforward cake and is an ideal way to make the most of rhubarb when it is in season.

Rhubarb and pistachio cake

Serves: 8–10

½ cup plus 3 tablespoons (150 g) butter, plus extra for greasing

⅔ cup (150 g) coconut yogurt

3 eggs, lightly beaten

5 tablespoons (100 g) honey

⅔ cup (100 g) rice flour

½ cup (50 g) cornstarch

⅓ cup (45 g) arrowroot

1 cup (100 g) ground pistachios

1 teaspoon baking powder

1 teaspoon baking soda

1 teaspoon vanilla extract

5⅓ oz. (150 g) rhubarb

Preheat the oven to 350°F (180°C). Grease and line an 8 by 4-inch (800 ml) loaf pan with parchment paper. Whisk all the ingredients, except the rhubarb, together until smooth. Pour the batter into the pan and top with the rhubarb.

Bake for 55 minutes until a skewer inserted in the center comes out clean. Cover loosely with foil after 30 minutes to avoid burning. Cool for 10 minutes in the pan and then turn out onto a wire rack.

Cake will keep for 1–2 days in the refrigerator, stored in an airtight container. Allow to come up to room temperature before serving.

10 min. / 20 min.

The hint of fragrant rose water and the crushed pistachio nuts create a delicate flavor, color, and texture, making these cupcakes the perfect cake for any party or celebration.

Raspberry, pistachio, and rose water cupcakes

Makes: 12

¾ cup plus 2 tablespoons (200 g) unsalted butter

⅔ cup (130 g) coconut sugar

3 eggs, lightly beaten

⅔ cup (100 g) rice flour

½ cup (50 g) cornstarch

⅓ cup (45 g) arrowroot

1 tablespoon baking powder

1¾ oz. (50 g) ground pistachios

3½ tablespoons (50 ml) milk

1½ teaspoons rose water

2¼ cups (300 g) raspberries

To decorate

Whipped Coconut Cream (see page 196)

Beet powder, for sprinkling

Preheat the oven to 350°F (170°C). Line a 12-cup cupcake pan with cupcake liners. In a bowl, whisk the butter and sugar until light and creamy. Add the eggs in batches, mixing well after each addition. Sift the flour, cornstarch, arrowroot, and baking powder, add the pistachios, and then gently fold into the wet mixture. Stir in the milk and rose water and then gently incorporate the raspberries.

Fill the cupcake liners two-thirds full and bake for 15 minutes. Remove from the oven and transfer to a wire rack to cool. Decorate with Whipped Coconut Cream and dust with beet powder.

Cupcakes will keep for 1–2 days in the refrigerator, stored in an airtight container. Allow to come up to room temperature before serving.

Banana and buckwheat loaf cake

Serves: 8–10

Oil or butter, for greasing

2 eggs, separated

3½ tablespoons (40 g) coconut sugar

2 ripe bananas, mashed

¾ cup (90 g) buckwheat flour

⅔ cup (100 g) cornstarch

1½ teaspoons baking powder

1 teaspoon ground cinnamon

½ teaspoon salt

Caramelized Banana Slices (see page 204), to serve

Preheat the oven to 350°F (170°C). Grease and line an 8 by 4-inch (800 ml) loaf pan with parchment paper. Whisk the egg yolks and sugar until light and fluffy. Add the mashed banana and whisk until evenly combined. Sift together all the dry ingredients and then fold in the egg mixture.

In another bowl, whisk the egg whites to stiff peaks and gently fold them into the batter until it is smooth. Pour the batter into the pan and bake for 25 minutes or until a skewer inserted into the center comes out clean. Leave it to cool in the pan for 5 minutes and then turn it out onto a wire rack to cool completely. Serve topped with the Caramelized Banana Slices.

This will keep well in an airtight container for up to 3 days, or it freezes well in slices.

10 min. / 1 hour

A simple vanilla cake with the extra flavor and moistness of the fruit baked inside.

Mixed berry cake

Serves: 10

1 cup plus 2 tablespoons (250 g) butter, plus extra for greasing
1 cup (160 g) rice flour
2/3 cup (80 g) cornstarch
2/3 cup (90 g) arrowroot
1 tablespoon baking powder
2 tablespoons honey
3/4 cup (150 g) coconut sugar
5 eggs, lightly beaten
2/3 cup (150 g) coconut yogurt
Seeds from 1 vanilla bean (see page 21)
2/3 cup (100 g) raspberries
2/3 cup (100 g) blueberries

Topping

9 oz. (250 g) crème fraîche
2/3 cup (100 g) raspberries
2/3 cup (100 g) blueberries

Preheat the oven to 350°F (170°C). Grease and line an 8-inch (20 cm) round cake pan with parchment paper. Sift the flour with the cornstarch, arrowroot, and baking powder. Whisk the butter, honey, and sugar until well combined. Add the eggs, a little at a time, beating well after each addition, and then fold in the flour mixture, yogurt, and vanilla.

Spoon half the batter into the pan and then gently stir the berries into the reserved half. Spoon the rest of the batter on top and bake for 1 hour or until cooked. Cool in the pan for 5 minutes and then turn out onto a wire rack to cool completely. Top with crème fraîche and mixed berries.

Cake will keep for 1–2 days in the refrigerator, stored in an airtight container. Allow to come up to room temperature before serving.

10 min. / 40 min.

A simple fruit like pear can get to another level when added to a cake, plus they come with the extra benefit of a good amount of fiber and vitamin C.

Pear and chocolate loaf cake

Serves: 8–10

7 tablespoons (100 g) butter, plus extra for greasing

1 cup (100 g) almond flour

½ cup (80 g) rice flour

⅓ cup (40 g) cornstarch

½ cup (50 g) raw cacao powder

½ cup (100 g) coconut sugar

3 eggs, lightly beaten

2 tablespoons plain yogurt

3 small pears, peeled

Preheat the oven to 350°F (180°C). Grease and line an 8 by 4-inch (800 ml) loaf pan with parchment paper. Sift together the flours, cornstarch, and cacao powder. Whisk the butter and sugar together. Add the eggs, a little at a time, beating well after each addition. Fold in the flours and yogurt. Pour into the pan and submerge the pears into the batter, standing them one after the other. Bake for 40 minutes.

Cake will keep for 1–2 days in the refrigerator, stored in an airtight container. Allow to come up to room temperature before serving.

15 min. / 1 hour

A twist on the classic American cheesecake, the ricotta gives this cake a unique flavor and makes it light and fluffy. Marbling with raspberry coulis swirl adds a wow factor.

Ricotta cheesecake

Serves: 10
1 Cheesecake Crust
(see page 115)

Filling
1 ripe banana, mashed
1lb. 2 oz. (500 g) ricotta
1 cup (250 g) sour cream
¼ cup (75 g) acacia honey
Grated zest of 1 lemon
1 tablespoon cornstarch
3 eggs, lightly beaten
2 tablespoons Raspberry Coulis (see page 200)

Press the Cheesecake Crust mixture into the base of an 8-inch (20 cm) round cake pan and chill. Preheat the oven to 300°F (150°C).

To make the filling, beat the banana, ricotta, sour cream, honey, lemon zest, and cornstarch together in a bowl until combined. Slowly add the eggs and mix thoroughly. Transfer the batter to the pan. Drizzle the Raspberry Coulis on top and create a swirl with a wooden toothpick or knife. Bake for 1 hour or until the filling has set. Let the cake cool completely before removing from the pan.

Cake will keep for 1–2 days in the refrigerator, stored in an airtight container. Allow to come up to room temperature before serving.

DAIRY ALTERNATIVES

Dairy in baking

Dairy products add moisture, richness, and flavor and promote leavening, making the final product light and soft. They also contribute to the consistency and color of the crust, maintaining the quality and nutritional value of baked products.

Milk alternatives

There are plenty of milk alternatives available. Milks like almond, cashew, oat, or coconut are mostly interchangeable in an equal amount, but of course you have to take into account the final result and see how the type of milk chosen will work with the other flavors in the recipe.

Cashew milk

67 calories

Nutrition per ½ cup (100 ml)

- 5.8 g fat
- 3.7 g carbohydrates
- 2 g protein

Oat milk

45 calories

Nutrition per ½ cup (100 ml)

- 1.5 g fat
- 6.5 g carbohydrates
- 1 g protein

Almond milk

40 calories

Nutrition per ½ cup (100 ml)

- 2 g fat
- 5 g carbohydrates
- 1 g protein

Rice milk

47 calories

Nutrition per ½ cup (100 ml)

- 1 g fat
- 4 g carbohydrates
- 0.1 g protein

Coconut milk

188 calories

Nutrition per ½ cup (100 ml)

- 20 g fat
- 2 g carbohydrates
- 1 g protein

Soy milk

40 calories

Nutrition per ½ cup (100 ml)

- 2 g fat
- 2 g carbohydrates
- 3.5 g protein

Dairy-free milk

almond milk

Made with either whole almonds or almond butter and water.

A nutritious, low-calorie drink, it is made by grinding almonds, mixing them with water, and then filtering the mixture to create a product that looks a lot like milk and has a sweet and nutty flavor.

cashew milk

Made from a mixture of cashew nuts or cashew butter and water.

Since the nuts are blended into the water, no nuts go to waste in the process and that means that the milk retains all of the fiber and nutrients present in the cashews. It is rich and creamy and has a sweet and subtle nutty flavor.

coconut milk

Made from the white flesh of brown coconuts.

Made by grating fresh coconut flesh and then working that with water, traditionally by hand. With little water added, rich coconut cream is obtained, while more water results in a thinner milk. It has a creamy texture and a sweet but subtle flavor.

oat milk

Made from a mixture of oats and water, but often extra ingredients such as gums, oils, and salt are added to produce a desirable taste and texture.

Oat milk is simply rolled oats and water blended together then strained to leave the pulp behind. It has a mild and sweet flavor.

rice milk

Made from milled white or brown rice and water, but can contain thickeners to improve texture and taste.

It is the most hypoallergenic non-dairy milk and it is mild in taste and naturally sweet in flavor with a slightly watery consistency.

soy milk

Made from soybeans and filtered water.

Because soy milk is a plant-based milk it is naturally free from cholesterol and low in saturated fat. Traditionally soy milk has a beany taste.

alternatives

Compared to cow's milk, it is low in calories, fat, and carbohydrates. It is a natural source of vitamin E, a group of antioxidants that help protect the body from disease-causing substances known as free radicals. On the other hand, almond milk is a much less concentrated source of the beneficial nutrients found in whole almonds, including protein, fiber, and healthy fats, as it is made up of mostly water.

Look for brands that contain a higher content of almonds, around 7–15%. Almond milk also contains phytic acid, a substance that limits the absorption of iron, zinc, and calcium.

Contains less than one-third of the calories of cow's milk, half the fat, and significantly less protein and carbohydrates.

The nut pulp is strained from the milk for the supermarket brands and so all the nutrients are lost. Cashew milk is one of the easiest milks to make at home.

Contains one-third the calories of cow's milk, half the fat, and significantly less protein and carbohydrates. High in medium-chain triglycerides (MCTs), a type of saturated fat.

The version in cartons sold alongside milk is a water-diluted version of the type of coconut milk usually sold in cans.

Contains a similar number of calories to cow's milk, up to double the number of carbohydrates, and about half the amount of protein and fat, but it is high in total fiber and beta-glucan, which can help lower cholesterol and blood sugar levels.

You can choose to add vanilla extract or Medjool dates to give it a bit more natural sweetness or raw cacao powder to make a chocolate oat milk.

Contains a similar number of calories to cow's milk and almost double the carbohydrates, but less protein and fat.

It also contains high levels of inorganic arsenic, which may cause some potential health problems in those who consume rice as a main food source.

It's a good source of protein, vitamin A, vitamin B-12, and potassium, plus it can be fortified with calcium and vitamin D. It contains as much protein as cow's milk, but is lower in calories than whole milk and about equal to the calories in skim milk. Some producers add thickeners to give it the mouthfeel of cow's milk.

Soy milk flavor quality differs according to the cultivar of soybean used in its production. Most soy milk in the supermarket is flavored and fortified with extra calcium and vitamins. The most popular flavors are vanilla and chocolate.

HOW TO MAKE CASHEW NUT MILK

This is a no-waste dairy-free alternative, since the nuts are blended entirely into the water, which means that the milk retains all the nutrients present in the nut, like magnesium, phosphorus, iron, potassium, and zinc.

Makes: 4¼ cups (1 liter)
PREP TIME: 10 min., plus 4 hours soaking

9 oz. (250 g) cashew nuts
4 cups (1 liter) filtered water

01 Soak the cashew nuts for 4 hours in a bowl with 2 cups (500 ml) of water.

02 Drain the cashew nuts.

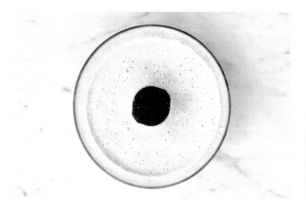

03 Place the nuts and the filtered water in a blender and blitz for 5 minutes.

04 Using a funnel, pour the milk into a clean bottle, seal, and keep in the fridge for 5 days.

HOW TO MAKE NUT BUTTER

To achieve the right consistency without adding liquid you need time and patience, as the whole process can take up to 30 minutes. You can also decide to use just one type of nut instead of a mixed selection.

Makes: 14 oz. (400 g)
PREP / COOK TIME: 12 min. / 30 min.

14 oz. (400 g) mixed almonds, walnuts, and hazelnuts
½ teaspoon salt

01 Preheat the oven to 350°F (170°C). Place the nuts on a baking tray and roast for 12 minutes.

02 Transfer the nuts to a clean dish towel and rub them against each other to remove the skin.

03 Place the nuts in a food processor and blend, scraping down the side as needed, until smooth and spreadable. Note that it will require 30 minutes.

04 Once ready add the salt, mix thoroughly, and transfer to a clean jar and store in the fridge for up to a month.

BUTTER ALTERNATIVES

Some butter alternatives have higher water contents, so cutting back a little on other liquids or adding a bit more flour will balance that out. The butter replacements most often used are in the form of nuts, nut butters, coconut butter, coconut oil, or vegetable oil.

coconut butter   633 calories
Nutrition per 3½ oz. (100 g)

- 63 g fat
- 6.6 g protein

nut butter (almond)   588 calories
Nutrition per 3½ oz. (100 g)

- 53.4 g fat
- 20.4 g protein

AMOUNT OF BUTTER/OIL		REPLACE WITH		WHY USE A BUTTER ALTERNATIVE?
3½ oz. (100 g) butter	→	3½ oz. (100 g) unsweetened apple purée	→	for added moistness
3½ oz. (100 g) butter	→	3½ oz. (100 g) bananas, mashed	→	results in a rich, dense texture that can be great for all kinds of sweets
3½ oz. (100 g) butter	→	1¾ oz. (50 g) avocado	→	best used in chocolate recipes as it will impart a green color to the bake
3½ oz. (100 g) butter	→	⅓ cup (80 ml) vegetable oil	→	strong flavor, works well in recipes that have a fruity or nutty quality
3½ oz. (100 g) butter	→	½ cup (120 ml) coconut oil	→	cuts down on saturated fats and won't change the flavor of food too much
1 cup (250 ml) oil	→	2 bananas, mashed	→	use low-gluten flour and reduce baking time
3½ oz. (100 g) butter	→	3½ oz. (100 g) plain yogurt	→	will give your baked goods a creamy and moist texture
3½ oz. (100 g) butter	→	1¾ oz. (50 g) nut butter + 3½ tablespoons (50 ml) coconut oil	→	will add nuttiness, but can make the baked goods denser

EASY SWAPS FOR CREAM IN BAKING

Plant-based dairy alternatives will surprise you with their light, delicate flavor when using them as replacements for yogurt, cream, and buttermilk. Coconut yogurt adds luxurious creaminess to frosting and moisture to cakes. Coconut milk can be whisked into a light cream to make mouthwatering mousses, cheesecakes, and icings. Cashew and macadamia nuts are perfect to create not only delicious milk, but also thick cream and yogurt to use in any icing.

TO CREATE THE PERFECT DAIRY-FREE BUTTERMILK

Add 2 tablespoons lemon juice or apple cider vinegar to 1 cup (240 ml) almond milk, or any plant-based milk, and leave for 15 minutes or until it curdles. Use as a 1:1 replacement for dairy buttermilk in your recipe.

AMOUNT OF CREAM		REPLACE WITH
1 cup (250 ml) any kind of cream	=	same amount of Cashew Nut Frosting (see page 202)
1 cup (250 ml) half-and-half	=	blend silken tofu until smooth and substitute using a 1:1 ratio OR blend ¾ cup (190 ml) rice milk with ¼ cup (60 ml) olive oil
1 cup (250 ml) heavy cream	=	same amount of coconut cream (refrigerate a can of full-fat coconut milk for several hours or overnight. The coconut cream will rise to the top and can easily be skimmed off) OR blend ¾ cup (165 ml) rice milk with ⅓ cup (80 ml) olive oil (but it will not whip)

EASY SWAPS FOR YOGURT IN BAKING

Cashew nuts—simply soak and blend into a thick cream with a yogurt-like consistency. Use in a 1:1 ratio.

Coconut cream—refrigerate a can of full-fat coconut milk for several hours or overnight. The coconut cream will rise to the top and can easily be skimmed off. Depending on your needs, coconut cream can substitute for yogurt in a 1:1 ratio. Be aware that coconut cream is much higher in fat than the other options listed.

Dairy-free yogurt—some people love to make dairy-free yogurt at home but it is often thinner than dairy yogurt. For the most part, shop-bought dairy-free brands work as an equivalent substitute yogurt, so you can substitute for yogurt using a 1:1 ratio.

Puréed silken tofu—a medium firm silken tofu will purée into a nice consistency and can substitute for yogurt using a 1:1 ratio.

15 min. / 30 min.

Beet is commonly combined with chocolate, as it masks any possible subtle earthy flavor, making this a simple way of adding antioxidants and nutrients to the recipe without sacrificing taste or texture.

Beet and chocolate cake

Serves: 10

Vegetable oil, for greasing

¾ cup (100 g) sorghum flour

⅓ cup (40 g) cornstarch

1 teaspoon baking powder

3 tablespoons (20 g) raw cacao powder, plus extra for dusting

9 oz. (250 g) cooked and peeled beets

7 oz. (200 g) Milk-Free Chocolate (see page 80)

¼ cup (60 ml) hot coffee

¾ cup (200 g) almond butter

5 eggs, separated

½ cup (120 ml) maple syrup

Preheat the oven to 350°F (180°C). Grease and line an 8-inch (20 cm) cake pan with parchment paper. Sift all the dry ingredients together. Purée the beets in a food processor or blender. Melt the chocolate in a heatproof bowl set over a pan of simmering water (making sure the bottom of the bowl doesn't touch the water), then pour in the coffee. Remove from the heat. Stir in the nut butter and mix to combine.

Whisk the egg yolks with the syrup in a bowl until frothy and then stir in the chocolate mixture. Fold in the beets and then the dry ingredients. Whisk the egg whites until stiff peaks form and fold into the chocolate mixture. Pour the batter into the pan and bake for 30 minutes or until a skewer inserted in the center comes out clean. Leave to cool in the pan. Dust with cacao powder to serve.

Cake will keep for 2–4 days in the refrigerator, stored in an airtight container. Allow to come up to room temperature before serving.

10 min. / 25 min.

These small cakes are perfect for those who find regular cupcakes a bit too sweet and prefer something more subtle. With a moist texture, these cupcakes also have a topping of creamy coconut icing.

Carrot cupcakes

Makes: 8

9 oz. (250 g) carrots, grated
1 teaspoon baking powder
1 teaspoon vanilla extract
2 eggs, lightly beaten
1 teaspoon ground cinnamon
½ teaspoon ground ginger
1 cup (100 g) almond flour
⅓ cup (50 g) rice flour
2 tablespoons (30 ml) coconut oil
5 tablespoons (75 ml) maple syrup
Whipped Coconut Cream (see page 196), to serve

Preheat the oven to 350°F (170°C). Place 8 cupcake liners in a 12-cup cupcake pan. Place all the ingredients in a large bowl and mix well until combined. Spoon the batter into the liners. Bake for about 25 minutes or until a skewer inserted in the center comes out clean. Leave to cool.

Decorate the cupcakes with the Whipped Coconut Cream when they are completely cool. Chill in the fridge for 1 hour before serving.

Cupcakes will keep for 1–2 days in the refrigerator, stored in an airtight container. Allow to come up to room temperature before serving.

10 min. / 35 min.

This Bundt cake is a bit denser than a standard sheet cake or layer cake, but it still manages to have a wonderfully soft texture at the same time.

Hazelnut Bundt cake

Serves: 10–12

Vegetable oil, for greasing
¾ cup (120 g) rice flour, plus extra for dusting
1 cup (250 g) almond butter
⅔ cup (150 ml) maple syrup
5 eggs
½ cup (65 g) cornstarch
½ cup (65 g) arrowroot
1 tablespoon baking powder
2 teaspoons baking soda
1¾ cups (150g) ground hazelnuts
½ cup (50g) chopped hazelnuts
⅔ cup (150 ml) almond milk

To decorate

2 tablespoons maple syrup
1 tablespoon chopped hazelnuts

Preheat the oven to 350°F (180°C). Grease and dust with rice flour an 8½-inch (22 cm) Bundt cake pan. Cream the almond butter and maple syrup together. Add the eggs, a little at a time, mixing well after each addition. Mix all the dry ingredients together, including the flour, and then gradually add to the butter mixture, alternating with the milk.

Transfer the cake batter into the pan and bake for 35 minutes or until a skewer inserted in the center comes out clean. Leave the cake to cool in the pan for 10 minutes and then turn out onto a wire rack to cool completely. Drizzle with maple syrup and decorate with hazelnuts before serving.

Cake will keep for 2–4 days in the refrigerator, stored in an airtight container. Allow to come up to room temperature before serving.

40 min. / 15 min.

Whole oranges puréed into the almond cake batter create an incredibly moist and fragrant sponge. Serve with a chocolate mousse to play on the classic pairing of chocolate and orange.

Orange, almond, and chocolate chip mini cakes

Makes: 12
2 oranges
Vegetable oil, for greasing
4 eggs
⅔ cup (130 g) coconut sugar
1¼ cups (125 g) ground almonds
1 cup (120 g) oat flour
2 teaspoons baking powder
Pinch of salt
5 oz. (150 g) dairy-free chocolate chips
Cacao Sauce (see page 220), to decorate

Place the oranges in a saucepan and cover with water. Bring to a boil and then simmer for 30 minutes until soft. Set aside. Preheat the oven to 350°F (170°C). Grease a 12-cup silicone mold.

When the oranges are cool, cut them in half, discard any seeds, and blend until smooth. Whisk the eggs and sugar until pale and then combine with the puréed orange. Add the dry ingredients and mix to combine. Stir in the chocolate chips and pour into the silicone mold. Bake for 15 minutes or until a skewer inserted in the center comes out clean. Prick the cakes all over with a toothpick and then pour the syrup over. Leave the cakes to cool in the pan. Pipe the Cacao Sauce on top of each cake to decorate.

Cakes will keep for 2–4 days in the refrigerator, stored in an airtight container. Allow to come up to room temperature before serving.

5 min. / 3 hours

This is a proper bittersweet chocolate made with only 4 ingredients and no added flavors or emulsifiers. Rich and intense, let it melt into your mouth to appreciate its strong flavor.

Milk-free chocolate block

Makes: 1 lb. 5 oz. (600 g)

Vegetable oil, for greasing
10½ oz. (300 g) cacao butter, chopped in small pieces
1⅓ cups (150 g) raw cacao powder
6 tablespoons (90 ml) maple syrup
Seeds from 1 vanilla bean (see page 21)

Grease and line a 15 x 10 x ¾-inch (38 x 25 x 2 cm) baking tray with parchment paper. Melt the cacao butter in a heatproof bowl set over a pan of simmering water (making sure the bottom of the bowl doesn't touch the water) until it reaches 104°F (40°C). Take care not to overheat, otherwise the chocolate will taste grainy and will have a white, cloudy appearance.

Remove from the heat, add the remaining ingredients, and use a handheld blender just to mix together, keeping the temperature at 82°F (28°C). Pour into the tray, tap gently to get rid of any air bubbles, and smooth the surface with a palette knife. Chill in the fridge for 3 hours. Break the chocolate into pieces.

Store in an airtight container in the fridge for up to 3 months.

This cheesecake is vibrant, simple to make, and ultra fresh with the perfect balance of sweetness and tartness. The crust is crunchy while the filling is super creamy, luscious, and rich, just perfect for summer.

Blackberry cheesecake

Serves: 10
1 Cheesecake Crust
(see page 115)

Filling
7 oz. (200 g)
blackberries
3 tablespoons (60 g)
honey
Seeds from 1 vanilla
bean (see page 21)
Grated zest and juice
of 1 lemon
1lb. 2 oz. (500 g)
Cashew Nut Frosting
(see page 202)

Preheat the oven to 350°F (180°C). Press the Cheesecake Crust mixture into the base of an 8-inch (20 cm) loose-bottom round cake pan and bake for 10 minutes.

To make the filling, put the blackberries in a saucepan with the honey and vanilla seeds. Set over medium heat and cook, stirring, for about 10 minutes until the mixture becomes sticky. Stir in the lemon juice and zest and set aside to cool.

In a bowl whisk the Cashew Nut Frosting and spread the soft cheese mixture over the crust until it is level. Chill for 2 hours. Top with the fruit mixture and then chill overnight.

Cake will keep for 1–2 days in the refrigerator, stored in an airtight container. Allow to come up to room temperature before serving.

10 min. / 22 min.

These cakes are moist and chocolatey, just like
any good red velvet cupcake should be, but they're
100% food coloring-free as their gorgeous red hue
comes from the addition of beet.

Red velvet cupcakes

Makes: 10

9 oz. (260 g) beets,
grated
2 eggs
1 teaspoon vanilla extract
½ teaspoon ground
cinnamon
pinch of sea salt
1½ cups (150 g) almond
flour
½ cup (80 g) rice flour
½ tablespoon baking
soda
3 tablespoons (20 g) raw
cacao powder
½ cup (100 g) coconut
sugar
3 tablespoons (45 ml)
coconut oil
1 teaspoon baking
powder
Freeze-fried raspberries,
to decorate
Whipped Coconut Cream
(see page 196), to serve

Preheat the oven to 350°F (170°C). Line a 12-cup cupcake pan
with 10 cupcake liners. Combine all the ingredients together in a
large bowl and mix well until combined.

Spoon into the liners and bake for 22 minutes or until a skewer
inserted in the center comes out clean. Remove from the oven
and leave to cool completely in the pan. Scatter with freeze-dried
raspberries and serve with the Whipped Coconut Cream, if desired.

Cupcakes will keep for 1–2 days in the refrigerator, stored in
an airtight container. Allow to come up to room temperature
before serving.

10 min. / 25 min.

These apple and almond mini loaf cakes truly are a heavenly combination. With the chunks of sweet apples nestled in a tender and fragrant blossom cake, they are the essence of simplicity.

Apple, almond, and orange blossom mini cakes

Makes: 4

Vegetable oil, for greasing
10½ oz. (300 g) apple, coarsely grated
2 eggs, lightly beaten
¼ cup (60 ml) coconut milk
2 tablespoons honey
2 teaspoons vanilla extract
1 teaspoon orange blossom water
1 cup (100 g) almond flour
⅔ cup (100 g) rice flour
⅓ cup (40 g) cornstarch
2 teaspoons baking powder
Dried apple slices, to decorate

Preheat the oven to 325°F (160°C). Grease and line 4 mini loaf pans with parchment paper. Place all the ingredients in a bowl and stir until just combined. Pour the batter into the pans and bake for 25 minutes or until a skewer inserted into the center comes out clean. Decorate with dried apple slices to serve.

Cakes will keep for 2–4 days in the refrigerator, stored in an airtight container. Allow to come up to room temperature before serving.

15 min. / overnight

This is a lovely, simple, no-bake dessert and very easy to make. It takes minutes to put together, and the only hard part is being patient for it to chill overnight so it can set.

Blueberry and lime cheesecake

Makes: 8
Vegetable oil, for greasing
⅔ cup (90 g) Medjool dates, pitted
1 teaspoon vanilla extract
¾ cup (70 g) desiccated coconut
1 teaspoon flaxseeds
2 tablespoons coconut oil
2 tablespoons maple syrup

Filling
12 oz. (350 g) blueberries
½ cup (100 ml) lime juice
Grated zest of 2 limes
⅓ cup (110 g) honey
7 oz. (200 g) Cashew Nut Frosting (see page 202)
⅓ cup (80 ml) coconut oil
9 oz. (240 g) Whipped Coconut Cream (see page 196)

To decorate
9 oz. (250 g) frozen blueberries

Grease and line the base and sides of an 8-inch (20 cm) springform cake pan with parchment paper. Combine the dates, vanilla, coconut, flaxseeds, oil, and maple syrup in a food processor and blitz until everything is combined. Press into the base of the pan and chill for at least 30 minutes.

Blend the blueberries, lime zest and juice, and honey in a food processor or blender. Add the Cashew Nut Frosting and blend together. Melt the coconut oil and add to the blueberry mixture. Fold in the Whipped Coconut Cream and lightly whisk, just to combine. Pour the filling over the prepared base until it is level. Chill for at least 4 hours or overnight. Top with blueberries to serve.

Cake will keep for 1–2 days in the refrigerator, stored in an airtight container. Allow to come up to room temperature before serving.

10 min. / 20 min.

These raspberry mini cakes are a simple almond and honey cake recipe, studded with fresh raspberries. Baked in a mini cake pan and simply dusted with powdered sugar, they are perfect for a chic afternoon tea.

Raspberry mini cakes

Makes: 12

Vegetable oil, for greasing
1½ cups (150 g) ground almonds
1¼ cups (150 g) quinoa flour
2 tablespoons tapioca flour
1 teaspoon baking powder
5 tablespoons (100 g) honey
½ cup (120 ml) coconut oil
1 teaspoon vanilla extract
4 eggs, separated
⅔ cup (160 ml) almond milk
9 oz. (250 g) raspberries
1 tablespoon powdered sugar, for dusting

Preheat the oven to 350°F (180°C). Grease and line a 12-cup mini cake pan with parchment paper. Mix the ground almonds, quinoa flour, tapioca, and baking powder together in a bowl. Whisk the honey, coconut oil, and vanilla extract until smooth and then add the egg yolks, one by one, until well combined. Beat the egg whites in a separate bowl until soft peaks form.

Add the wet mix to the dry mix, along with the milk and two-thirds of the raspberries, and fold to combine. Fold in the egg whites and divide evenly into the mini cake pan. Place 1 or 2 raspberries on top of each cake. Bake for 20 minutes or until a skewer inserted in the center comes out clean. Dust with powdered sugar.

Cakes will keep for 1–2 days in the refrigerator, stored in an airtight container. Allow to come up to room temperature before serving.

10 min. / 35 min.

Using polenta instead of flour means you will create a different texture and the poppy seeds will add a nice speckled effect.

Orange, polenta, and poppy seed cake

Serves: 10–12

Vegetable oil, for greasing

3 eggs

5 tablespoons (100 g) honey

¼ cup (50 g) coconut sugar

Grated zest and juice of 2 oranges

5 tablespoons (75 ml) sunflower oil

1 cup (100 g) almond flour

⅔ cup (100 g) polenta

⅓ cup (50 g) rice flour

½ cup (65 g) cornstarch

½ oz. (15 g) poppy seeds, toasted

1 teaspoon baking powder

Syrup

Juice of 2 oranges, plus the peel, julienned

4 teaspoons (30 g) honey

Preheat the oven to 350°F (170°C). Grease and line an 8-inch (20 cm) cake pan with parchment paper. Combine all the ingredients in a bowl until smooth. Pour into the pan and bake for 35 minutes or until golden brown on top and a skewer inserted in the center comes out clean. Leave to cool in the pan.

To make the syrup, heat the orange juice and peel with the honey for a few minutes. Prick the cooled polenta cake with a toothpick all over and then pour the syrup over.

Cake will keep for 2–4 days in the refrigerator, stored in an airtight container. Allow to come up to room temperature before serving.

15 min. / 25 min.

Carrot cake freshened with orange juice and zest and texture from pistachios come together to make a grown-up carrot cake. Chantilly Cream is a lighter topping than traditional cream cheese frosting.

Carrot, orange, and pistachio cake

Serves: 8

Vegetable oil, for greasing
2 eggs
½ cup (100 g) coconut sugar
1½ cups (150 g) grated carrots
¾ cup (100 g) quinoa flour
⅓ cup (30 g) almond flour
1 teaspoon baking powder
½ teaspoon ground nutmeg
½ teaspoon ground cinnamon
Juice of 1 orange
Grated zest of 2 oranges
½ cup (30 g) pistachios, roughly chopped, plus extra to decorate
Chantilly Cream (see page 198), to decorate

Preheat the oven to 350°F (180°C). Grease and line a 7-inch (18 cm) cake pan with parchment paper. Whisk the eggs and sugar together and then add the carrots. Mix the other ingredients together in a separate bowl and then gently fold in the egg mixture.

Pour the batter into the pan and bake for 25 minutes or until the top springs back and a skewer inserted in the center comes out clean. Leave to cool for 5 minutes and then turn out onto a wire rack to cool completely. Decorate with the Chantilly Cream and some chopped pistachios.

Cake will keep for 1–2 days in the refrigerator, stored in an airtight container. Allow to come up to room temperature before serving.

20 min. / overnight

These little cheesecakes couldn't get easier. They feature an easy base crust, smooth and creamy lemon cashew cream filling, and a simple topping of frozen blueberries.

Blueberry and lemon mini cheesecakes

Makes: 10

1 Cheesecake Crust
(see page 115)
3½ oz. (100 g) frozen
blueberries, to decorate

Filling
⅔ cup (100 g) cashew
nuts, soaked in cold
water for 4 hours
⅓ cup (80 ml)
coconut oil
½ cup (120 ml) maple
syrup
Grated zest and juice
of 1 lemon
7 oz. (200 g) Whipped
Coconut Cream
(see page 196)

Grease an 8-cup silicone mold (use two or make in batches). Press the Cheesecake Crust into the molds and bake according to the recipe on page 115.

To make the filling, strain the cashew nuts and blend in a food processor until as fine as possible. Add the coconut oil and blend again. Add all the other ingredients and blend until combined. Fill the molds and chill overnight. Unmold just before serving and top with frozen blueberries.

Cakes will keep for 1–2 days in the refrigerator, stored in an airtight container. Allow to come up to room temperature before serving.

10 min. / 50 min.

This indulgent, fudgy cake is an insanely delicious, decadent dessert that you would never know had avocado in it. Made with no butter, it is topped with a rich nutty spread, fresh figs, and pistachios.

Chocolate avocado cake

Serves: 8

Vegetable oil, for greasing
10½ oz. (300 g) walnuts
5 oz. (150 g) avocado, pitted and peeled
1⅓ cups (200 g) dates, pitted and chopped
3 eggs
Seeds from 1 vanilla bean (see page 21)
4½ oz. (120 g) Whipped Coconut Cream (see page 196)
½ cup (100 g) coconut sugar
¾ cup (60 g) raw cacao powder
2 teaspoons baking powder
Hazelnut and Chocolate Spread (see page 206)
4 figs, quartered
1 teaspoon chopped pistachios

Preheat the oven to 350°F (180°C). Grease and line a 7-inch (18 cm) cake pan with parchment paper. In a food processor, combine the walnuts, avocado, and dates and process to a paste. In a bowl, whisk the eggs, vanilla, Whipped Coconut Cream, and sugar together and then add the date mixture.

Sift the cacao and baking powder together and then add to the batter. Bake for 50 minutes. Turn out onto a wire rack to cool before decorating with the Hazelnut and Chocolate Spread, fresh figs, and chopped pistachios.

Cake will keep for 1–2 days in the refrigerator, stored in an airtight container. Allow to come up to room temperature before serving.

dairy- and gluten-free

10 min. / 25 min.

These coconut and chocolate cakes may be "mini" but they have the taste of a cake giant. Fluffy chocolate sponge full of coconut is spread with silky and rich, nutty frosting and topped with toasted coconut.

Chocolate and coconut mini loaf cakes

Makes: 5

Vegetable oil, for greasing

2½ cups (230 g) desiccated coconut

2½ cups (600 ml) coconut milk

3 eggs

¾ cup (150 g) coconut sugar

1 tablespoon vanilla extract

⅔ cup (75 g) coconut flour

1⅓ cups (160 g) oat flour

1¼ cups (160 g) cornstarch

1 tablespoon baking powder

2½ oz. (75 g) Milk-Free Chocolate (see page 80), melted

To decorate

Fudge Frosting (see page 218)

2 tablespoons toasted coconut flakes

Preheat the oven to 350°F (170°C). Grease 5 mini loaf pans. Soak the desiccated coconut in the milk for 10 minutes. Whisk the eggs, sugar, and vanilla together and then add to the soaked coconut. Fold in the flours, cornstarch, baking powder, and chocolate.

Spoon into the pans and bake for 25 minutes or until cooked. Let the cakes cool in the pans for 10 minutes and then carefully turn out onto a wire rack to cool completely. Decorate with Fudge Frosting and coconut.

Cakes will keep for 2–4 days in the refrigerator, stored in an airtight container. Allow to come up to room temperature before serving.

dairy-, gluten-, and egg-free

Lighter and more delicate in texture than its New York counterpart, this green tea cheesecake is one true piece of sheer decadence. It's gluten- and dairy-free and rich in antioxidants and protein.

Kiwi and matcha tea cheesecake

Serves: 8
3½ tablespoons (50 ml) coconut oil, melted
1 cup (140 g) almonds
10 Medjool dates, pitted
½ cup (50 g) desiccated coconut

Filling
6 oz. (180 g) coconut cream
¾ cup (180 ml) coconut milk
½ cup (100 ml) lemon juice
5 tablespoons (70 ml) maple syrup
2 teaspoons Matcha powder
Seeds from 1 vanilla bean (see page 21)
½ cup (120 ml) coconut oil

Topping
3–4 kiwi fruits, peeled and sliced

Line a 7-inch (18 cm) springform cake pan with parchment paper. Place the coconut oil, almonds, dates, and coconut in a food processor or blender and blend until the mixture resembles breadcrumbs. Press into the base of the pan.

Blend all the filling ingredients together until smooth and creamy. Pour over the crust and chill in the fridge overnight. Decorate with the sliced kiwi before serving.

Cake will keep for 1–2 days in the refrigerator, stored in an airtight container. Allow to come up to room temperature before serving.

35 min. / 40 min.

This cake is super quick to make with the exception of cooking the whole clementines, which you can do ahead of time if you want. You can use any kind of small citrus fruit for this cake.

Clementine, honey, and olive oil cake

Serves: 10–12

Vegetable oil, for greasing

13½ oz. (380 g) clementines

3 eggs

6 tablespoons (125 g) honey

3½ tablespoons (50 ml) olive oil

1½ cups (150 g) ground almonds

⅔ cup (100 g) cornstarch

⅔ cup (100 g) polenta

1 teaspoon baking powder

1 tablespoon powdered sugar

Preheat the oven to 325°F (160°C). Grease and line a 9½-inch (24 cm) cake pan with parchment paper. Place the clementines in a saucepan and cover with water, bring to a boil, and then simmer gently for 25 minutes over low heat. Drain and leave to cool. When cool enough, cut in half, remove any seeds and blend with the skins in a food processor or blender until smooth.

Add the eggs, honey, and olive oil, blending to combine. Add the almonds, cornstarch, polenta, and baking powder and blend just until mixed. Pour the batter into the cake pan, smoothing the top, and bake for 40 minutes or until a skewer comes out clean. Leave to cool in the pan and turn out onto a wire rack to cool completely. Dust with powdered sugar before serving.

Cake will keep for 2–4 days in the refrigerator, stored in an airtight container. Allow to come up to room temperature before serving.

12 min. / 10 min, plus chilling

A sweet and creamy cheesecake can be quite
a rich, heavy dish so it is nice to be able to balance
that against the natural flavors of mango and the
sharpness of the passion fruit.

Passion fruit and mango cheesecake

Serves: 8
1 Cheesecake Crust
(see page 115)

Filling
1½ oz. (45 g) passion
fruit
10½ oz. (300 g) mango,
pureed
3 oz. (80 g) Cashew Nut
Frosting (see page 202)
⅓ cup (75 ml) maple
syrup
⅓ cup (80 ml) coconut
oil, melted
1 cup (100 g) ground
almonds

Fruit Compote
2 passion fruit
1 mango,
peeled and diced

Preheat the oven to 350°F (180°C). Press the Cheesecake Crust
mixture into the base of a 7-inch (18 cm) cake pan and bake for
10 minutes.

To make the filling, cut the passion fruit and scoop the insides into
a pan. Add the mango and cook over low heat for 10 minutes
until thickened. Remove from the heat and leave to cool. Mix the
Cashew Nut Frosting, syrup, and oil and blend until smooth. Fold
into the mango mixture together with the almonds, pour over the
crust, and chill overnight.

To make the compote, cut the passion fruit in half and scoop the
insides into a bowl. Add the mango and mix together. Pour the
compote on top of the cream layer and chill until ready to serve.

Cake will keep for 1–2 days in the refrigerator, stored in an airtight
container. Allow to come up to room temperature before serving.

dairy- and gluten-free

10 min. / 45 min.

This recipe, made using grated organic orange, lemon, and lime zest, gives an extra citrus hint to your cake. Eaten for breakfast, this cake will turn your mornings into a glorious moment.

Citrus yogurt Bundt cake

Serves: 10–12

¾ cup plus 2 tablespoons (215 ml) sunflower oil, plus extra for greasing
4 eggs
1 cup (200 g) coconut sugar
½ cup (120 ml) maple syrup
1½ cups (325 g) coconut yogurt
¾ cup plus 2 tablespoons (135 g) rice flour
½ cup (65 g) cornstarch
½ cup (65 g) arrowroot
4 teaspoons (20 g) baking powder
2 teaspoons grated lemon zest
2 teaspoons grated orange zest
2 teaspoons grated lime zest
Powdered sugar, for dusting

Preheat the oven to 350°F (170°C). Grease a 9½-inch (23 cm) Bundt cake pan. Whisk the eggs and sugar until pale. Add the maple syrup, yogurt, and oil and stir to mix. Sift in the flour, cornstarch, arrowroot, baking powder, and citrus zests and mix.

Pour into the pan and bake for 45 minutes until golden and dry inside. Remove from the oven and leave to cool for 5 minutes. Turn out onto a wire rack to cool completely. Dust with icing sugar before serving.

Cake will keep for 2–4 days in the refrigerator, stored in an airtight container. Allow to come up to room temperature before serving.

FLOUR ALTERNATIVES

Flour in baking

Flour provides volume and structure.
When the flour proteins combine with
moisture and heat, they turn into gluten
and gluten helps to bring the ingredients
together, creating a structure to which
starches adhere.

oat flour   420 calories
**Nutrition per
¾ cup (100 g)**

- 9.5 g fat
- 68 g carbohydrates
- 15 g protein

almond flour   648 calories
**Nutrition per
1 cup (120 g)**

- 56 g fat
- 24 g carbohydrates
- 24 g protein

polenta
Nutrition per
¾ cup (100 g)

370 calories

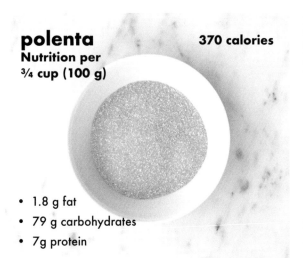

- 1.8 g fat
- 79 g carbohydrates
- 7g protein

buckwheat flour
Nutrition per
1 cup (120 g)

402 calories

- 3.7 g fat
- 85 g carbohydrates
- 15 g protein

coconut flour
Nutrition per
1 cup (120 g)

532 calories

- 21g fat
- 63 g carbohydrates
- 22.4 g protein

white rice flour
Nutrition per
¾ cup (120 g)

366 calories

- 1.42 g fat
- 80.1 g carbohydrates
- 5.95 g protein

quinoa flour
Nutrition per
1 cup (125 g)

440 calories

- 8 g fat
- 88 g carbohydrates
- 16 g protein

sorghum flour
Nutrition per
1 cup (125 g)

434 calories

- 4 g fat
- 93 g carbohydrates
- 10 g protein

Gluten-free flours

Learning how to bake gluten-free is overwhelming when starting out, but the key is to create the best texture using a combination of flours and starches as shown here.

light flours (starches)

- Arrowroot is a powder extracted from a combination of several plant rootstocks and is easy to digest.

- Cornstarch is milled from corn into a fine white powder.

- Potato starch has a great ability to add moisture.

- Xanthan gum is produced through the fermentation of sucrose, glucose, and lactose and what is left from the fermentation is then dried and ground into a fine powder. It is very useful in egg-free baking.

- Baking powder/baking soda are leavening agents or baking aids, which help to create a good rise and add lightness. They are not interchangeable.

medium flours (nutritious)

- Millet flour comes from the grass family and has a dry and nutty flavor. It has a protein content similar to whole wheat flour.

- Oat flour is rich in vitamins and fiber and provides a nice even flavor and a great rise to cakes. It can be used alone or in combination with other flours.

- Quinoa is related to the plant family of spinach and beets and, despite its very distinct flavor, it is a great medium based flour that can work alone or in combination with other flours. It is full of minerals and vitamins and produces a great texture.

- Sorghum flour imitates the texture and lightness of wheat flour and gives great tenderness to baked goods.

- White rice flour is light and has a very bland taste, but gives great results and this is why it is a common flour in a blend.

- Polenta is milled from dried corn kernels and has a rich yellow color, ranging in texture from fine to coarse.

heavy flours (dense and nutritious)

- Ground nut flour (e.g. almond) is a great way to give cake a buttery flavor, adding richness and moisture.

- Amaranth flour is made from the seeds of the amaranth plant, a leafy vegetable. It is denser and more nutritious than most flours.

- Brown rice flour is very comparable to whole wheat flour with its dense nutrition and great structure, but is best to use in super fine-ground form to avoid that gritty texture. It has a pleasant nutty flavor.

- Buckwheat is related to rhubarb, has a strong nutty flavor, and can give cakes a nice brown shade. It is full of nutrition and density.

- Coconut flour is made from dried, defatted coconut meat. It is high in fiber with a light coconut flavor and a great way of absorbing the liquid in a recipe, which is why it needs to be used in small amounts.

- Teff flour comes from the grass family and has a unique flavor. It is light, but creates a dense texture at the same time, so it is best if used in smaller amounts.

blended flour combinations

The more variety of flours you have in your blend, the more amazing results you can achieve. You could experiment and use a different combination every time to find the one that you like the most. Every flour has its own characteristics, so start with replacing the same amount of all-purpose flour.

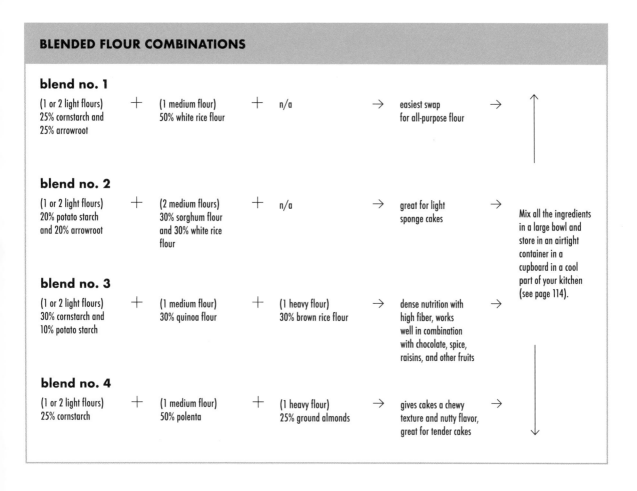

BLENDED FLOUR COMBINATIONS

blend no. 1

| (1 or 2 light flours) 25% cornstarch and 25% arrowroot | + | (1 medium flour) 50% white rice flour | + | n/a | → | easiest swap for all-purpose flour | → | |

blend no. 2

| (1 or 2 light flours) 20% potato starch and 20% arrowroot | + | (2 medium flours) 30% sorghum flour and 30% white rice flour | + | n/a | → | great for light sponge cakes | → | Mix all the ingredients in a large bowl and store in an airtight container in a cupboard in a cool part of your kitchen (see page 114). |

blend no. 3

| (1 or 2 light flours) 30% cornstarch and 10% potato starch | + | (1 medium flour) 30% quinoa flour | + | (1 heavy flour) 30% brown rice flour | → | dense nutrition with high fiber, works well in combination with chocolate, spice, raisins, and other fruits | → | |

blend no. 4

| (1 or 2 light flours) 25% cornstarch | + | (1 medium flour) 50% polenta | + | (1 heavy flour) 25% ground almonds | → | gives cakes a chewy texture and nutty flavor, great for tender cakes | → | |

HOW TO MAKE BLENDED GLUTEN-FREE FLOUR

The bonus of using a blend of alternative flours is that many of them have unique and delicious flavors, which can enhance the recipe. This particular blend adds great texture and structure to baked goods.

Makes: 2¼ lb. (1 kg)

PREP TIME: 5 minutes

1 cup (300 g) sorghum flour

2 cups (300 g) white rice flour

1½ cups (200 g) potato starch

1½ cups (195 g) arrowroot

01 Weigh all the different flours.

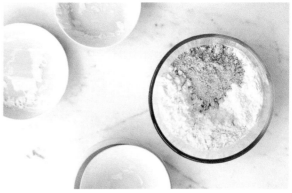

02 Place the flours in a large bowl and mix well to combine.

03 Store the flour blend in an airtight container in a dry, dark place.

04 Shake the container before using in case the flour has settled.

HOW TO MAKE A CHEESECAKE CRUST

A great alternative to the classic cheesecake crust full of sugar, this recipe bursts with natural flavors and is packed with antioxidants, fiber, high protein, and healthy fats.

Makes: an 8-inch (20 cm) cheesecake crust or 8 small cheesecakes

PREP / COOK TIME: 10 min. / 12 min.

- 2 oz. (60 g) whole almonds
- ⅔ cup (80 g) oat flour
- 3 tablespoons (40 g) coconut sugar

- Pinch of salt
- 2 tablespoons coconut oil, melted

- 1 tablespoon + 1 teaspoon (20 g) maple syrup
- ¾ oz. (20 g) desiccated coconut

01 Preheat the oven to 350°F (180°C). Put the almonds on a baking tray and roast for 5 minutes until fragrant, then place them with the oat flour, sugar, and salt in a food processor.

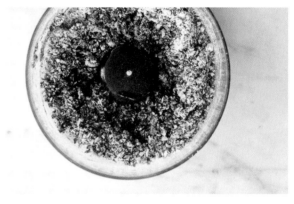

02 Finely grind the almonds. Add the wet ingredients and blend again, scraping down the side. Add the desiccated coconut and mix thoroughly.

03 Place the mixture in the lined pan and press down evenly with the help of a glass.

04 Bake for 12 minutes until lightly browned and set aside to cool.

10 min. / 35 min.

This cake can be iced with a simple cashew icing or dusted with powdered sugar. Blueberries have a mild flavor but are packed with a good amount of antioxidants, phytonutrients, and fiber.

Blueberry Bundt cake

Serves: 10–12

½ cup (120 ml) sunflower oil, plus extra for greasing

1 cup (100 g) teff flour, plus extra for dusting

3 eggs

½ cup (120 ml) maple syrup

Seeds from 1 vanilla bean (see page 21)

¾ cup (100 g) quinoa flour

⅓ cup (50 g) rice flour

1 tablespoon baking powder

¼ cup (60 ml) milk

3½ oz. (100 g) blueberries

Icing

1 tablespoon beet powder

1 tablespoon blueberry powder

Cashew Nut Frosting (see page 202)

Preheat the oven to 350°F (180°C). Grease a 9½-inch (23 cm) Bundt cake pan and lightly dust with flour. In a large bowl, whisk the eggs, maple syrup, and vanilla seeds until combined. Slowly add the oil while still whisking. Combine the flours and baking powder and then add to the egg mixture, alternating with the milk, until well mixed. Gently fold in the blueberries.

Transfer the cake batter to the pan and bake for 35 minutes or until a skewer inserted in the center comes out clean. Leave to cool in the pan for 10 minutes and then turn out onto a wire rack to cool completely. Mix the beet and blueberry powders with the frosting and drizzle over the cake to serve.

Cake will keep for 2–4 days in the refrigerator, stored in an airtight container. Allow to come up to room temperature before serving.

20 min. / 18 min.

In Italy, chestnut flour has been known for centuries as sweet flour because if you put a pinch of chestnut flour on your tongue it is like chewing into a sweet and dry chestnut.

Carrot mini cakes

Makes: 8

Vegetable oil, for greasing

⅓ cup (50 g) rice flour, plus extra for dusting

1 cup (100 g) chestnut flour

½ cup (40 g) almond flour

⅓ cup (60 g) cornstarch

1 teaspoon baking powder

4 eggs, separated

1 cup (200 g) coconut sugar

9 oz. (260 g) carrots, grated

1 teaspoon ground cinnamon

Seeds from 1 vanilla bean (see page 21)

¾ cup (60 g) desiccated coconut

1 teaspoon ground ginger

To serve

1 cup (250 g) Greek yogurt

1 tablespoon julienned lemon zest

Preheat the oven to 350°F (180°C). Grease and dust an 8-cup mini cake pan with flour. Mix the flours, cornstarch, and baking powder together. Whisk the egg yolks with the sugar until combined. Fold in the remaining ingredients, except the egg whites.

In a bowl, whisk the egg whites until stiff peaks form and then gently fold in the cake batter. Transfer to the mini cake pan and bake for 18 minutes or until a skewer inserted in the center comes out clean. Cool down in the pan for 5 minutes and then turn out onto a wire rack to cool completely. Serve with Greek yogurt and decorate with lemon zest.

Cakes will keep for 2–4 days in the refrigerator, stored in an airtight container. Allow to come up to room temperature before serving.

10 min. / 40 min.

This traditional German apple cake recipe is really easy to make. With a simple batter that rises up and bakes around the apples, this is the perfect everyday dessert that tastes best with a dollop of cream on top.

German apple cake

Serves: 10

½ cup (113 g) butter, plus extra for greasing
4 eggs, separated
¾ cup (150 g) coconut sugar
1 teaspoon vanilla extract
1⅔ cups (250 g) rice flour
Grated zest of 1 lemon
2 teaspoons baking powder
⅔ cup (150 ml) milk
3 apples, thinly sliced
1 tablespoon honey
1 teaspoon ground cinnamon
Whipped Coconut Cream (see page 196), to serve

Preheat the oven to 350°F (180°C). Grease and line an 8-inch (20 cm) springform cake pan with parchment paper. Whisk the egg yolks, butter, sugar, and vanilla extract together. Add the rice flour, lemon zest, baking powder, and milk and whisk to combine. In a bowl, whisk the egg whites to stiff peaks and then gently fold into the batter.

Pour the batter into the pan. Arrange the apple slices on top. Bake for 40 minutes or until a skewer inserted in the center comes out clean. Leave to cool in the pan for 10 minutes and then turn out onto a wire rack. Brush with honey and dust with cinnamon before serving with a dollop of whipped cream, if desired.

Cake will keep for 2–4 days in the refrigerator, stored in an airtight container. Allow to come up to room temperature before serving.

10 min. / 15 min.

The buckwheat in this recipe has a strong flavor that tends to blend better with more earthy flavors, such as chocolate.

Chocolate buckwheat cupcakes

Makes: 10

⅔ cup (50 g) raw cacao powder, plus extra for dusting

½ cup (120 ml) boiling water

¾ cup (175 g) unsalted butter, softened

1 teaspoon vanilla extract

½ cup (100 g) coconut sugar

3 eggs, lightly beaten

¾ cup (90 g) buckwheat flour

1 teaspoon baking powder

½ teaspoon xanthan gum

Chantilly Cream (see page 198), to serve

Preheat the oven to 350°F (180°C). Line a 12-cup cupcake pan with 10 cupcake liners. Set aside. Sift the cacao powder into a bowl, pour in the boiling water, and mix to a thick paste. Whisk the butter, vanilla, and sugar until light and fluffy and then add the eggs, a little at a time. Add the flour, baking powder, xanthan gum, and cacao mixture and whisk until combined.

Divide the batter equally among the 10 paper liners and bake for 15 minutes until well risen and springy to the touch. Cool in the liners on a wire rack. Decorate with Chantilly Cream and dust with cacao powder before serving.

Cakes will keep for 2–4 days in the refrigerator, stored in an airtight container. Allow to come up to room temperature before serving.

10 min. / 25 min.

Don't miss out on a classic recipe like Victoria sponge cake just because you're avoiding gluten. This easy recipe is just perfect with your favorite jam and a dusting of powdered sugar.

Victoria sponge cake

Serves: 10–12

Vegetable oil, for greasing
4 eggs, lightly beaten
Seeds from 1 vanilla bean (see page 21)
2 tablespoons rice milk
1 cup plus 2 tablespoons (250 g) butter, softened
½ cup (100 g) coconut sugar
¾ cup (120 g) rice flour
⅓ cup (60 g) cornstarch
½ cup (65 g) arrowroot
2 teaspoons baking powder

Filling

1 cup (250 ml) whipping cream
1 teaspoon vanilla extract
1 teaspoon cornstarch

To layer

1 recipe Mixed Berry and Vanilla Jam (see page 208)
1 tablespoon powdered sugar, for dusting

Preheat the oven to 350°F (180°C). Grease and line two 8-inch (20 cm) springform cake pans with parchment paper. Mix the eggs, vanilla, and milk together. Whisk the butter and sugar until fluffy, then gradually add the egg mixture. Combine the flour, cornstarch, arrowroot, and baking powder and then add to the cake batter, stirring only briefly.

Divide the batter between the cake pans and bake for 25 minutes or until a skewer inserted in the center comes out clean. Cool in the pan for 10 minutes and then turn out onto a wire rack to cool completely.

To make the filling, whip the cream with the vanilla and cornstarch until stiff. Place one cake on a serving plate, spread the jam evenly on the surface, and then top with the cream. Place the second cake on top and press down lightly to join the two. Dust with powdered sugar.

Cake will keep for 1–2 days in the refrigerator, stored in an airtight container. Allow to come up to room temperature before serving.

15 min. / 40 min.

Raspberries are such a treat in late summer and autumn. They hold their flavor and texture well in a cake and add a dash of bright color. If raspberries are out of season, try using frozen berries instead.

Raspberry and banana loaf cake

Serves: 8–10

Vegetable oil, for greasing

3 eggs, lightly beaten

10 tablespoons (120 g) coconut sugar

12 oz. (350 g) mashed banana

½ cup (120 ml) sunflower oil

½ cup (120 ml) almond milk

¾ cup (100 g) quinoa flour

⅔ cup (100 g) brown rice flour

⅔ cup (10 g) cornstarch

¼ cup (40 g) potato starch

2 teaspoons baking powder

7 oz. (200 g) raspberries

To decorate

2 tablespoons Mixed Berry and Vanilla Jam (see page 208)

1¾ oz. (50 g) raspberries

1 tablespoon desiccated coconut

Preheat the oven to 350°F (180°C). Grease and line an 8 by 4-inch (800 ml) loaf pan with parchment paper. Whisk the eggs and sugar together and then add the banana, oil, and milk. Combine all the dry ingredients together and make a well in the center. Pour the egg mixture into the well and stir to combine. Gently fold in the raspberries.

Transfer the cake batter to the loaf pan and bake for 40 minutes or until a skewer inserted in the center comes out clean. Leave to cool in the pan for 5 minutes before turning, top side up, onto a wire rack to cool completely. Brush with jam and decorate with raspberries and coconut before serving.

Cake will keep for 1–2 days in the refrigerator, stored in an airtight container. Allow to come up to room temperature before serving.

30 min. / 50 min.

Mixing the pulpy orange into the batter makes this cake incredibly moist with a flavor that is marmalade-like; perfect for people who prefer a bit of bitterness and complexity in their cakes.

Whole-orange cake

Serves: 10–12

2 large oranges,
roughly chopped

Vegetable oil, for greasing

5 eggs, separated

½ cup (100 g)
coconut sugar

3½ tablespoons (50 ml)
maple syrup

1 cup (150 g) polenta

1½ cups (150 g) ground
almonds

2 teaspoons baking
powder

Glaze

2 tablespoons powdered
sugar

1 tablespoon lemon juice

Place the oranges in a saucepan, cover with water, and simmer for 20 minutes. Set aside to cool. Preheat the oven to 350°F (180°C). Grease a 9½-inch (23 cm) Bundt cake pan. Blend the oranges in a food processor or blender until finely puréed.

Whisk the egg yolks and sugar until thick and then whisk in the puréed orange and maple syrup. Gradually add the polenta, ground almonds, and baking powder. In another bowl, whisk the egg whites until stiff peaks form. Add 3 tablespoons of egg whites to loosen up the almond mixture and then gently fold in the remaining whites.

Transfer the cake batter to the cake pan and bake for 35 minutes until a skewer inserted in the center comes out clean. Remove from the oven and leave to cool for 10 minutes and then leave to cool completely on a rack. Mix the powdered sugar and lemon juice to a paste and drizzle it over the cake before serving.

Cake will keep for 2–4 days in the refrigerator, stored in an airtight container. Allow to come up to room temperature before serving.

15 min. / 25 min.

Here is a super simple, finger-licking recipe for a beet and date chocolate cake packed with antioxidants, cancer-beating properties, whole grains, fiber, magnesium-rich cacao, and vitamin C.

Beet and cacao mini loaf cakes

Makes: 4

¼ cup (60 ml) sunflower oil, plus extra for greasing

¾ cup (120 g) rice flour

½ cup (85 g) cornstarch

⅔ cup (90 g) arrowroot

½ cup (60 g) buckwheat flour

⅓ cup (25 g) raw cacao powder

1 tablespoon baking powder

2 oz. (55 g) Date Paste (see page 20)

3 eggs, lightly beaten

12 oz. (350 g) banana, mashed

8 oz. (230 g) canned beets, drained and puréed

½ cup (120 ml) maple syrup

To serve

Greek yogurt

Caramelized Plums (see page 204)

Preheat the oven to 350°F (180°C). Grease 4 mini loaf cake pans. Sift the dry ingredients together and then stir in all the other ingredients. Stir until combined. Pour into the mini pans and bake for 25 minutes or until a skewer inserted in the center comes out clean. Leave to cool in the pans for 5 minutes and then turn out onto a wire rack to cool completely. Serve with yogurt and caramelized plums, if desired.

Cakes will keep for 2–4 days in the refrigerator, stored in an airtight container. Allow to come up to room temperature before serving.

dairy- and gluten-free

10 min. / 45 min.

A great source of fiber and full of vitamins and minerals, baked figs can take your cakes up a level. Known for being a healthy and versatile ingredient, they add a burst of sweetness.

Fig and cinnamon loaf cake

Serves: 8–10

¼ cup (60 ml) sunflower oil, plus extra for greasing

1 cup (160 g) rice flour

½ cup (85 g) cornstarch

⅔ cup (90 g) arrowroot

2 teaspoons baking powder

1 teaspoon ground cinnamon

½ cup (120 ml) maple syrup, plus extra for brushing

3 eggs, lightly beaten

12 oz. (350 g) mashed banana

7 figs—4 chopped and 3 halved

Preheat the oven to 350°F (180°C). Grease and line an 8 by 4-inch (800 ml) loaf cake pan with parchment paper. In a bowl, sift the flour, cornstarch, arrowroot, baking powder, and cinnamon together. In another bowl, mix all the other ingredients, except the halved figs. Combine the wet and dry mixtures and then transfer to the loaf pan.

Gently place the halved figs on top and bake for 45 minutes or until a skewer inserted in the center comes out clean. Leave to cool in the pan for 5 minutes and then turn out onto a wire rack to cool completely. Brush with maple syrup before serving.

Cake will keep for 2–4 days in the refrigerator, stored in an airtight container. Allow to come up to room temperature before serving.

40 min. / 25 min.

These individual delicious mini chocolate cakes are light and fudgy all at once; served with fresh figs and chopped pistachios, they are an impressive and elegant dessert for a special dinner.

Buckwheat and chocolate fudge mini cakes

Serves: 10

Vegetable oil for greasing
3½ oz. (100 g) prunes, pitted
¾ cup plus 2 tablespoons (200 g) unsalted butter, softened
½ cup (100 g) coconut sugar
2 eggs
1 teaspoon vanilla extract
1¾ oz. (50 g) Date Paste (see page 20)
3½ oz. (90 g) 70% chocolate, melted
¾ cup (100 g) buckwheat flour
⅔ cup (50 g) raw cacao powder
⅓ cup (50 g) cornstarch
2 teaspoons baking powder

To decorate

Cacao Sauce
(see page 220)
4 figs, sliced
1 tablespoon chopped pistachios

Preheat the oven to 350°F (170°C). Grease 10 mini loaf cake pans (or bake in batches). Soak the prunes for 30 minutes in the ½ cup (100 ml) boiling water. Blitz the butter, sugar, and soaked prunes with their water in a food processor or blender until smooth. Add the eggs and vanilla and blitz until evenly combined. Add the Date Paste and then the melted chocolate and mix. Add the dry ingredients and blitz until the batter is smooth.

Pour the batter into the mini pans and smooth over the tops with a spatula. Bake for 25 minutes until set on top—be aware that a metal skewer should not come out clean. Leave to cool in the pan. Decorate with Cacao Sauce, sliced figs, and pistachios.

Cakes will keep for 2–4 days in the refrigerator, stored in an airtight container. Allow to come up to room temperature before serving.

10 min. / 55 min.

The combination of mango and coconut works so beautifully.

Mango and coconut loaf cake

Serves: 8–10

Vegetable oil, for greasing

¾ cup (90 g) sorghum flour

½ cup (80 g) rice flour

¼ cup (40 g) potato starch

⅓ cup (45 g) arrowroot

2 teaspoons baking powder

¼ cup (50 g) coconut sugar

½ cup (40 g) desiccated coconut

3 eggs, lightly beaten

⅓ cup (80 ml) maple syrup

11 oz. (320 g) mashed banana

7 oz. (200 g) mango, roughly chopped

1 teaspoon vanilla extract

¼ cup (60 ml) coconut oil

1 recipe Mango Curd (see page 212)

Preheat the oven to 350°F (180°C). Grease and line an 8 by 4-inch (800 ml) loaf pan with parchment paper. Sift the dry ingredients together and then add all the other ingredients except the Mango Curd. Pour into the pan and bake for 55 minutes or until a skewer inserted in the center comes out clean. Cool in the pan for 5 minutes and then turn out onto a wire rack. Serve with the Mango Curd.

Cake will keep for 2–4 days in the refrigerator, stored in an airtight container. Allow to come up to room temperature before serving.

10 min. / 55 min.

Considered an ancient grain, amaranth is a great source of nutrition. It has a mild flavor and is slightly nutty and toasty.

Amaranth, chocolate, and sour cherries cake

Serves: 10–12

¾ cup (200 ml) sunflower oil, plus extra for greasing
5 eggs
1 teaspoon vanilla extract
¾ cup (150 g) coconut sugar
6 oz. (175 g) amaranth
½ cup (75 g) cornstarch
1½ cups (150 g) ground almonds
5 teaspoons baking powder
¾ cup (180 ml) coconut milk
3½ oz. (100 g) Milk-Free Chocolate (see page 80), roughly chopped
7 oz. (200 g) sour cherries, frozen and thawed
Cacao Sauce (see page 220), for serving

Preheat the oven to 350°F (180°C). Grease a 9½-inch (23 cm) Bundt cake pan and lightly dust with flour. Whisk the eggs, vanilla extract, and sugar until smooth. While whisking, add the oil. Mix all the dry ingredients together and then add them in batches to the egg mixture, alternating with the coconut milk.

Gently fold in the chocolate and cherries. Transfer the cake batter to the pan and bake for 55 minutes or until a skewer inserted in the center comes out clean. Leave to cool in the pan for 10 minutes and then turn out onto a wire rack to cool completely. Pour the Cacao Sauce over the top before serving.

Cake will keep for 2–4 days in the refrigerator, stored in an airtight container. Allow to come up to room temperature before serving.

10 min. / 25 min.

A small version of a classic recipe with the addition of aromatic orange blossom water. The result is fragrant and moist and the citrus slices add a sweet final touch.

Almond, polenta, and orange blossom mini cakes

Makes: 8

¾ cup plus 2 tablespoons (200 g) butter, softened, plus extra for greasing

1 tablespoon orange zest

1 tablespoon orange blossom water

½ cup (100 g) coconut sugar

3 eggs

1½ teaspoons baking powder

⅓ cup (150 g) cornstarch

⅔ cup (100 g) polenta

1 cup (100 g) almond flour

Juice of 2 oranges

½ cup (100 ml) milk

2 tablespoons maple syrup

Maple Glazed Citrus Slices (see page 214), for serving

Preheat the oven to 350°F (170°C). Grease 8 cups of a 12-cup mini cake pan. Whisk the butter, orange zest, orange blossom water, and sugar until light and creamy. Gradually add the eggs and beat well. Sift the baking powder with the cornstarch in a bowl and then add the polenta and almond flour and mix together. Add to the butter mixture and then add the orange juice and milk. Stir to combine and spoon into the pan.

Bake for 25 minutes or until a skewer inserted in the center comes out clean. Drizzle with syrup and top with the Maple Glazed Citrus Slices to serve.

Cakes will keep for 2–4 days in the refrigerator, stored in an airtight container. Allow to come up to room temperature before serving.

10 min. / 18 min.

Simply remove a small section of the sponge and fill with jam for a delightful surprise hidden inside your mini cakes.

Buckwheat and red berry mini cakes

Makes: 18

4 teaspoons (20 ml) sunflower oil, plus extra for greasing

7 eggs, separated

¾ cup (150 g) coconut sugar

1⅔ cups (200 g) buckwheat flour

1½ cups (150 g) ground almonds

1 teaspoon baking powder

10½ oz. (300 g) Mixed Berry and Vanilla Jam (see page 208)

1 tablespoon powdered sugar

Preheat the oven to 350°F (180°C). Grease two 12-cup mini cake pans (or bake in batches). Whisk the egg yolks with the sugar until combined. While still whisking, slowly add the oil. Mix together the buckwheat flour, ground almonds, and baking powder and then add to the egg mixture. In another bowl, whisk the egg whites until stiff peaks form. Gently fold in the egg mixture.

Pour the batter into the pan and bake for 18 minutes or until a skewer inserted in the center comes out clean. Leave to cool for 10 minutes in the pan and then turn out onto a wire rack to cool completely. Remove the center of each cake with an apple corer and fill with jam. Dust with the powdered sugar to serve.

Cakes will keep for 2–4 days in the refrigerator, stored in an airtight container. Allow to come up to room temperature before serving.

10 min. / 60 min.

A classic marble cake will always be a welcome feature at afternoon tea. This version is wonderfully rich, moist, and filled with little pieces of apricot.

Apricot and chocolate marble loaf cake

Serves: 8–10

1 cup plus 2 tablespoons (250 g) butter, plus extra for greasing

5 tablespoons (60 g) coconut sugar

3 tablespoons (65 g) honey

4 eggs, lightly beaten

3½ tablespoons (50 ml) maple syrup

¾ cup (120 g) rice flour

⅓ cup (55 g) cornstarch

⅓ cup (45 g) arrowroot

1½ teaspoons baking powder

½ teaspoon xanthan gum

2 tablespoons raw cacao powder

⅓ cup (50 g) dried apricots, finely chopped

Preheat the oven to 350°F (180°C). Grease and line an 8 by 4-inch (800 ml) loaf pan with parchment paper. Whisk the butter, sugar, and honey together until light and fluffy. Add the eggs in small batches, whisking well after each addition. Add the syrup. Sift in the flour, cornstarch, arrowroot, baking powder, and xanthan gum and whisk to combine.

Divide the batter between 2 bowls. Add the cacao to one bowl and apricots to the other, mixing well. Pour the chocolate batter into the pan and then the apricot batter. Use a spatula to lightly swirl the two batters together. Bake for 1 hour until a skewer inserted in the center comes out clean. Leave to cool in the pan for 10 minutes and then turn out onto a wire rack to cool completely.

Cake will keep for 2–4 days in the refrigerator, stored in an airtight container. Allow to come up to room temperature before serving.

10 min. / 35 min.

This traditional Italian cake is named after the island of Capri. It is a flourless chocolate cake enriched with ground almonds that make it a perfect choice for those in search of gluten-free desserts.

Caprese cake

Serves: 10

½ cup plus 1 tablespoon (125 g) butter, plus extra for greasing

5 oz. (150 g) dark chocolate, roughly chopped

3 eggs, separated

½ cup (100 g) coconut sugar

2 cups (185 g) ground almonds

1 tablespoon raw cacao powder

Preheat the oven to 350°F (170°C). Grease and line an 8-inch (20 cm) springform cake pan with parchment paper. Melt the chocolate and butter in a heatproof bowl set over a pan of simmering water (making sure the bottom of the bowl doesn't touch the water) and set aside. Whisk the egg yolks with the sugar until combined and then add in the chocolate mixture and almonds.

In another bowl, whisk the egg whites until stiff peaks form and then gently fold in the chocolate mixture. Transfer the batter to the pan and bake for 35 minutes or until just set and the cake springs back lightly when touched. Remove from the oven and leave to cool in the pan. Dust with cacao powder.

Cake will keep for 2–4 days in the refrigerator, stored in an airtight container. Allow to come up to room temperature before serving.

10 min. / 35 min.

This cake has a sharp lemon flavor, but the cardamom brings a subtle undertone that really gives depth to the flavor without taking away any of the tartness from the lemon.

Cardamom and lemon drizzle loaf cake

Serves: 8–10

Vegetable oil, for greasing
½ cup (150 g) sorghum flour
⅓ cup (50 g) rice flour
¼ cup (35 g) cornstarch
¼ cup (40 g) potato starch
1½ teaspoons baking powder
¾ cup plus 2 tablespoons (175 g) butter, softened
¾ cup (175 g) coconut sugar
1 tablespoon green cardamom pods, seeds removed and crushed in a mortar and pestle
Grated zest and juice of 1 lemon
3 eggs, lightly beaten

Drizzle

Grated zest and juice of 1 lemon
1 tablespoon powdered sugar

Preheat the oven to 350°F (180°C). Grease and line an 8 by 4-inch (800 ml) loaf pan with parchment paper. Sift together the flour, cornstarch, potato starch, and baking powder. Whisk the butter, sugar, crushed cardamom seeds, and lemon zest and juice until combined. Add the beaten eggs in a few batches. Gently fold in the flour.

Pour the batter into the pan and bake for 35 minutes or until a skewer inserted in the center comes out clean. Remove the cake from the oven and make holes in the top with a skewer. Mix the lemon zest and juice with the powdered sugar and spoon it over the top, letting it seep through the holes. Leave to cool completely in the pan.

Cake will keep for 2–4 days in the refrigerator, stored in an airtight container. Allow to come up to room temperature before serving.

20 min. / 18 min.

Indulge a little with these squidgy mini chocolate treats. This is a rich dark chocolate recipe with the addition of prunes; a super-moist chocolate cake that everyone will love.

Almond, prune, and chocolate mini bites

Makes: 18

Vegetable oil, for greasing

5 oz. (140 g) prunes, pitted

⅓ cup (75 ml) hot water

2 teaspoons vanilla extract

5 oz. (150 g) Milk-Free Chocolate (see page 80), broken into pieces

6 tablespoons (100 g) almond butter

4 eggs, separated

7 tablespoons (80 g) coconut sugar

2 tablespoons maple syrup

1¼ cups (125 g) ground almonds

2 tablespoons raw cacao powder, for dusting

Preheat the oven to 350°F (170°C). Grease an 8-cup silicone mold (bake in batches). Simmer the prunes in the hot water with the vanilla for 5 minutes and then blitz in a food processor or blender to make a smooth paste. Melt the chocolate and almond butter in a heatproof bowl set over a pan of simmering water (making sure the bottom of the bowl doesn't touch the water) and then stir in the prune paste.

Whisk the egg yolks with the sugar and maple syrup until well combined. Fold in the chocolate mixture and the almonds. Whisk the egg whites until soft peaks form and then gently fold into the cake batter. Pour into the pan and bake for 18 minutes. Leave to cool completely in the pan. Remove from the pan and dust with cacao powder.

Bites will keep for 2–4 days in the refrigerator, stored in an airtight container. Allow to come up to room temperature before serving.

10 min. / 22 min.

Mixing quinoa flour with almond, chocolate, and cherry brings this simple cake to another level. It's packed with high protein, healthy fats, fiber, and minerals.

Cherry and chocolate chip cake

Serves: 10

½ cup plus 1 tablespoon (125 g) butter, softened, plus extra for greasing
¾ cup (100 g) oat flour
½ cup (60 g) quinoa flour
1 cup (100 g) almond flour
1 tablespoon baking powder
1 teaspoon vanilla extract
½ cup (100 g) coconut sugar
3 eggs, lightly beaten
4¼ oz. (120 g) mashed bananas
½ cup (100 ml) milk
3½ oz. (100 g) sour cherries
1 oz. (30 g) Milk-Free Chocolate (see page 80), roughly chopped
1 tablespoon powdered sugar

Preheat the oven to 350°F (180°C). Grease and line a 9-inch (23 cm) square cake pan with parchment paper. Sift the flours and baking powder together. Whisk the butter, vanilla extract, and sugar until combined. Add the eggs in batches and then add the bananas. Fold in the dry ingredients gradually, alternating with the milk. Gently fold in the cherries and chocolate.

Transfer the batter to the pan and bake for 22 minutes or until a skewer inserted in the center comes out clean. Leave to cool in the pan for 10 minutes and then turn out onto a wire rack to cool completely. Dust with powdered sugar before serving.

Cake will keep for 2–4 days in the refrigerator, stored in an airtight container. Allow to come up to room temperature before serving.

10 min. / 15 min.

With a rich chocolate and chestnut sponge and a light coconut filling, this stunning cake will have everyone coming back for seconds.

Chocolate and coffee roulade

Serves: 10

Vegetable oil, for greasing

5 eggs, separated

½ cup plus 3 tablespoons (135 g) coconut sugar

7 tablespoons (35 g) raw cacao powder

⅓ cup (35 g) chestnut flour

½ cup (75 g) Medjool dates, pitted

3 tablespoons espresso coffee, cooled

Seeds from 1 vanilla bean (see page 21)

1⅓ cups (310 ml) coconut cream

½ recipe Cacao Sauce (see page 220)

1 tablespoon chopped hazelnuts

Preheat the oven to 350°F (180°C). Grease and line a 15 x 10 x ¾-inch (38 x 25 x 2 cm) baking tray with parchment paper. Whisk the egg yolks and sugar together for 3–4 minutes until light and fluffy. Sift the cacao powder and flour and fold in carefully. In another bowl, whisk the egg whites until soft peaks form and then fold into the batter in three stages. Transfer the batter to the pan and bake for 15 minutes or until the surface springs back when gently pressed and the cake starts shrinking from the sides. Prepare the roulade sponge for rolling following the instructions on page 42.

Put the dates, coffee, and vanilla into a food processor or blender and blitz until fine. Add the coconut cream and blitz again until smooth and creamy. Fill and roll the roulade following the instructions on page 42. Lift onto a serving plate with the seam underneath and remove the paper. Drizzle with the Cacao Sauce and scatter the hazelnuts over the top before serving.

Roulade will keep for 1–2 days in the refrigerator, stored in an airtight container. Allow to come up to room temperature before serving.

15 min. / 35 min.

A rustic cake topped with fresh sliced pears, this simple cake is a showstopper in appearance and flavor. It is moist, flavor-packed, and beautiful with the pear slices baked in a decorative pattern on top.

Pear and walnut cake

Serves: 10

¾ cup (175 g) butter, diced, plus extra for greasing

1 cup (100 g) walnuts

½ cup (60 g) oat flour

½ cup (60 g) sorghum flour

3 tablespoons (20 g) cornstarch

½ cup (100 g) coconut sugar

2 eggs, lightly beaten

1¾ oz. (50 g) dark chocolate, roughly chopped

4 small ripe pears, sliced

Glaze

2 tablespoons honey

2 tablespoons water

Preheat the oven to 325°F (160°C). Grease and line a 9-inch (23 cm) square cake pan with parchment paper. Grind the walnuts in a food processor until fine and combine with the flours, cornstarch, and sugar. Add the butter and pulse until it forms crumbs and then add the eggs, mixing briefly. Gently fold in the chocolate.

Pour the batter into the pan and smooth the top. Place the sliced pears on the top, pushing them slightly into the batter, and bake for 35 minutes or until firm to the touch. Leave it to cool in the pan for 10 minutes and then turn out onto a wire rack to cool completely.

To make the glaze, mix the ingredients together and then brush it over the cooled cake.

Cake will keep for 2–4 days in the refrigerator, stored in an airtight container. Allow to come up to room temperature before serving.

30 min. / 35 min.

This recipe using the whole lemon, pith and all, is full of deep citrus flavor and the almond flour gives this cake a dense richness.

Lemon and rice flour cake

Serves: 10

2 lemons

Vegetable oil, for greasing

6 eggs

⅔ cup (130 g) coconut sugar

¾ cup (120 g) rice flour

1¼ cups (125 g) ground almonds

2 teaspoons baking powder

¼ teaspoon salt

Glaze

2 tablespoons honey

2 tablespoons water

Place the lemons in a saucepan and cover with water. Bring to a boil, lower the heat, and simmer for 30 minutes. Set aside to cool. Preheat the oven to 350°F (180°C). Grease and line an 8-inch (20 cm) cake pan with parchment paper. When the lemons are cool, cut them in half and discard any seeds. Place the lemons in a food processor or blender and blitz until smooth.

Whisk the eggs and sugar until pale and thick. Mix in the puréed lemons. Add the dry ingredients and mix to combine. Pour the batter into the pan and bake for 35 minutes until a skewer inserted in the center comes out clean.

In a small saucepan, add the honey and water and simmer for a few minutes. Remove the cake from the oven and brush the glaze over the cake.

Cake will keep for 2–4 days in the refrigerator, stored in an airtight container. Allow to come up to room temperature before serving.

EGG ALTERNATIVES

Eggs in baking

Eggs add moisture to recipes and also have a leavening function, as adding air to a batter when combined with other acidic ingredients makes the cake light and soft.

Egg alternatives

It is possible to replace egg with other ingredients that provide moisture and lightly bind the other ingredients together.

flaxseed
Nutrition per
⅓ cup (50 g)

267 calories

- 21 g fat
- 15 g carbohydrates
- 9 g protein
- 14 g fiber

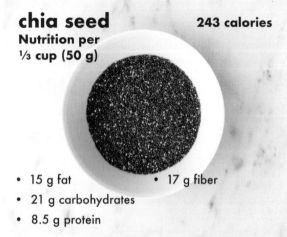

chia seed
Nutrition per
⅓ cup (50 g)

243 calories

- 15 g fat
- 21 g carbohydrates
- 8.5 g protein
- 17 g fiber

agar
Nutrition per 1 tablespoon (15 g)

14 calories

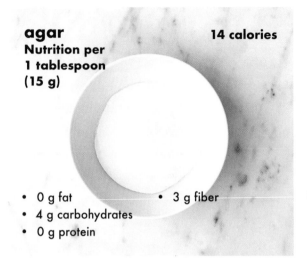

- 0 g fat
- 4 g carbohydrates
- 0 g protein
- 3 g fiber

vinegar
Nutrition per 7 tablespoons (100 g)

22 calories

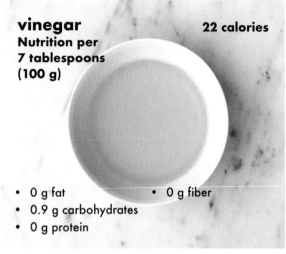

- 0 g fat
- 0.9 g carbohydrates
- 0 g protein
- 0 g fiber

nut butter
Nutrition per 3 tablespoons (50 g)

329 calories

- 27.7 g fat
- 9.4 g carbohydrates
- 10 g protein
- 2.1 g fiber

arrowroot
Nutrition per ⅓ cup (50 g)

178 calories

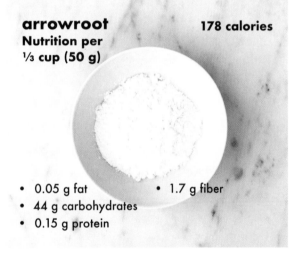

- 0.05 g fat
- 44 g carbohydrates
- 0.15 g protein
- 1.7 g fiber

potato flour
Nutrition per ⅓ cup (50 g)

178 calories

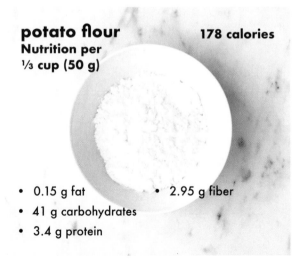

- 0.15 g fat
- 41 g carbohydrates
- 3.4 g protein
- 2.95 g fiber

yogurt
Nutrition per 3 tablespoons (50 g)

34 calories

- 1.7 g fat
- 1.8 g carbohydrates
- 1.9 g protein
- 0 g fiber

How to replace eggs

flaxseeds

1 egg = 1 tablespoon flaxseeds + 3 tablespoons (45 ml) water	Whisk together and let sit for 15 minutes before use.	Adds density and a subtle nuttiness and helps with leavening, binding, and moisture.

chia seeds

1 egg = 1 tablespoon chia seeds + ⅓ cup (80 ml) water	Combine and let sit for 15 minutes before use.	Adds a dark color and a very subtle poppy seed flavor and helps with binding and moisture. You could grind the seeds if you don't want to see them in the cake.

fruit

1 egg = 9 oz. (250 g) applesauce OR 1 mashed banana	Also increase the leavening agent by 50%. May need more baking time (10 min. or as much as needed).	The fruit will add sweetness and extra moisture to the final product. There will be a hint of apple or banana flavor, so if your recipe already includes banana or applesauce, use a different substitute. It helps with moisture and binding.

baking soda and vinegar

1 egg = 1 teaspoon baking soda + 1 tablespoon apple cider vinegar + ¼ cup (60 ml) extra liquid	Add the baking soda to the dry ingredients and the apple cider vinegar to the wet ingredients when following the original recipe.	This method is the best way to retain the original taste and texture when replacing eggs. These ingredients react with each other to form bubbles that expand during cooking to provide a light, fluffy texture.

nut butter

1 egg = 3 tablespoons (50 g) nut butter	Whisk the nut butter with the fat or sugar in the recipe.	Has a nutty, noticeable flavor and aroma, so use in any recipe where a nutty flavor is desirable. It helps with binding, moisture, and texture.

in baking

arrowroot powder

1 egg = 1 tablespoon arrowroot powder + 2 tablespoons water	Combine and then use.	This egg substitute is a great binder and moistening agent, but does not act as a leavening agent and therefore you need to combine with a proper leavening agent.

potato flour

1 egg = 1 tablespoon potato flour + 2 tablespoons water + ½ teaspoon baking powder + ¼ cup (60 ml) extra liquid	Combine all ingredients together and then use.	Like all the other starches, potato starch works to bind and add texture to baked goods.

agar

1 egg = 1 tablespoon agar + ¼ cup (60 ml) water	Combine and let sit for 15 minutes before use.	Gelatin will take on the flavor of other ingredients, helps with binding, and creates a smoother texture than flaxseed or chia seeds.

yogurt

1 egg = ¼ cup (65 g) plain yogurt + ½ teaspoon baking powder	You can also use soy yogurt if needed.	Natural yogurt mimics the richness of the egg, lending a wonderful creaminess to the baked goods.

HOW TO MAKE APPLE PURÉE

You can flavor the apple purée with ½ teaspoon ground cinnamon or ½ teaspoon vanilla extract.

Makes: 2¼ lb. (1 kg)

PREP / COOK TIME:
10 min. / 15 min.

3 lb. (1.4 kg) apples, washed, cored, and quartered

¼ cup (60 ml) water

01 Preheat the oven to 350°F (180°C). Place the apples on a baking tray and bake for about 20 minutes or until soft and golden brown.

02 Alternatively, place the apples and water in a small saucepan, cover, and cook for 15 minutes.

03 Transfer the boiled or baked apples to a food processor or blender and blitz until smooth, adding about 6 tablespoons water to the baked apples if using that method.

04 Use immediately or keep in a jar in the fridge for 5 days. You can also freeze the apple purée in small batches.

HOW TO MAKE CASHEW NUT "YOGURT"

dairy-, gluten-, and egg-free

Cashew nut "yogurt" has a thick, creamy, velvety texture combined with a nutty flavor. It's so easy to make and because the nuts are blended into the water, all the nutrients, like magnesium and zinc, are still present.

Makes: 10½ oz. (300 g)
PREP TIME: 10 minutes, plus 4 hours soaking

1 cup (150 g) cashew nuts
½ cup (120 ml) almond milk

Juice of 1 lemon
Seeds from 1 vanilla bean (see page 21)

01 Soak the cashew nuts in 1¼ cups (300 ml) water for 4 hours.

02 Drain the nuts and transfer to a food processor or blender with the almond milk, lemon juice, and vanilla seeds.

03 Blitz on high speed for a few minutes, scraping down the sides if necessary, until smooth and creamy.

04 Use immediately or transfer to an airtight container and keep in the fridge for 5 days.

15 min. / 30 min.

A great alternative to a creamy cake, chocolate cake, or fruit cake, this marmalade cake is ideal at teatime. The tangy cake made with dark marmalade and coconut sugar gives the perfect hint of fruitiness.

Marmalade loaf cake

Serves: 8–10

Vegetable oil, for greasing
½ cup (113 g) butter, diced
¾ cup (120 g) rice flour
⅓ cup (55 g) cornstarch
⅓ cup (45 g) arrowroot
7 tablespoons (80 g) coconut sugar
Grated zest of 1 orange
Grated zest of 1 lemon
1 teaspoon allspice
3½ oz. (100 g) candied citrus peel, currants, and raisins
Juice of 1 orange
3 tablespoons orange marmalade
½ cup (130 g) plain yogurt
Caramelized Orange (see page 204), to decorate

Preheat the oven to 350°F (180°C). Grease and line an 8 by 4-inch (800 ml) loaf pan with parchment paper. In a bowl, rub the diced butter into the flour, cornstarch, and arrowroot until the mixture resembles breadcrumbs. Add all the other dry ingredients and mix well. In a separate bowl, combine all the wet ingredients and then quickly pour over the flours and stir until well mixed.

Transfer the batter to the pan, level the surface, and bake for 30 minutes or until a skewer inserted in the center comes out clean. Leave to cool into the pan for 10 minutes and then turn out onto a wire rack to cool completely. Decorate with the Caramelized Orange slices.

Cake will keep for 2–4 days in the refrigerator, stored in an airtight container. Allow to come up to room temperature before serving.

10 min. / 13 min.

These sweet vanilla mini cakes will make everyone happy because they're not only healthy and nutritious, but delightfully tasty. The plum slices bring vibrant color and rich flavor to the cake.

Vanilla mini cakes

Makes: 12

Vegetable oil, for greasing
½ cup (60 g) buckwheat flour
⅓ cup (50 g) rice flour
3 tablespoons (30 g) potato starch
¼ cup (30 g) arrowroot
1 tablespoon baking powder
½ teaspoon salt
⅓ cup (65 g) coconut sugar
1 teaspoon vanilla extract
2 tablespoons sunflower oil
1 tablespoon apple cider vinegar
½ cup (120 ml) water
2 plums, thinly sliced
1 tablespoon powdered sugar, for dusting

Preheat the oven to 350°F (180°C). Grease a 12-cup cupcake pan. Sift the flours, potato starch, arrowroot, baking powder, and salt into a bowl and then stir in the sugar. In another bowl, combine all remaining ingredients, except the plums, with the water. Add the wet ingredients to the flour and beat until you have a smooth batter.

Pour the batter into the cupcake pan until each hole is about three-quarters full. Top with the sliced plums. Bake for 13 minutes or until risen and firm to the touch. Leave to cool completely before dusting with powdered sugar.

Cakes will keep for 2–4 days in the refrigerator, stored in an airtight container. Allow to come up to room temperature before serving.

15 min. / 25 min.

This light eggless apple cake, with a hint of cinnamon, is absolutely divine served warm with whipped coconut cream. The secret of its moistness is the addition of homemade apple purée (see page 164).

Apple cake

Serves: 10

Vegetable oil, for greasing
2 apples, peeled, cored, and sliced
1 tablespoon lemon juice
½ cup plus 1 tablespoon (125 g) butter, softened
6 tablespoons coconut sugar
⅔ cup (150 g) Apple Purée (see page 164)
¾ cup (120 g) rice flour
⅓ cup (55 g) cornstarch
⅓ cup (45 g) arrowroot
2 teaspoons baking powder
½ teaspoon salt
5 tablespoons (75 g) milk
1 teaspoon ground cinnamon
1 tablespoon maple syrup
Whipped Coconut Cream (see page 196), for serving

Preheat the oven to 350°F (170°C). Grease and line an 8-inch (20 cm) round cake pan with parchment paper. Coat the apple slices in the lemon juice and set aside. In a bowl, whisk the butter and sugar until pale and fluffy. Add the apple purée and beat until smooth. Sift the flour, cornstarch, arrowroot, baking powder, and salt and then add to the batter. Slowly add the milk, mixing well after each addition, until you have a smooth batter.

Transfer the batter to the pan and arrange the apple slices on top in a spiral pattern. In a bowl, mix the cinnamon and maple syrup together and then drizzle over the cake. Bake for 25 minutes or until a skewer inserted in the center comes out clean. Leave to cool for 15 minutes in the pan and then turn it out onto a wire rack. Serve with the Whipped Coconut Cream.

Cake will keep for 2–4 days in the refrigerator, stored in an airtight container. Allow to come up to room temperature before serving.

These egg-free chocolate mini Bundt cakes are easy, moist, and delicious, packed with flavor and just the right amount of chocolate.

Chocolate mini Bundt cakes

Makes: 24

Vegetable oil, for greasing
2 cups (300 g) Medjool dates, pitted
1¼ cups (300 ml) warm water
6 oz. (180 g) mashed banana
2 teaspoons vanilla extract
2 tablespoons flaxseeds
2 cups (200 g) spelt flour
1 oz. (30 g) cornstarch
⅔ cup (50 g) raw cacao powder, plus extra for dusting
1 teaspoon baking powder
1 teaspoon baking soda

Preheat the oven to 350°F (170°C). Grease a 6-cup mini Bundt cake pan (and bake in batches). Place the dates, warm water, banana, and vanilla in a food processor or blender and blitz until smooth. Mix the flaxseeds with 6 tablespoons (89 ml) water and let sit for a few minutes. In a large bowl, sift the flour, cornstarch, cacao powder, and baking powder and soda.

Pour the date and flaxseed mixture over the dry ingredients and whisk to combine. Pour the batter into the pan and bake for 15 minutes (baking in batches) or until set on top. Leave to cool in the pan. Dust with cacao powder before serving.

Cakes will keep for 2–4 days in the refrigerator, stored in an airtight container. Allow to come up to room temperature before serving.

10 min. / 23 min.

This is a light and moist-textured eggless "naked" cake, packed with vanilla flavor and topped with fresh fruits. It's a real showstopper, perfect to celebrate any occasion.

Vanilla celebration cake

Serves: 8

½ cup (100 ml) vegetable oil, plus extra for greasing
1⅓ cups (200 g) rice flour
⅔ cup (100 g) cornstarch
⅔ cup (100 g) arrowroot
1 cup (200 g) coconut sugar
1½ teaspoons baking soda
¼ teaspoon salt
1½ tablespoons apple cider vinegar
Seeds from 1 vanilla bean (see page 21)
2 cups (450 ml) milk

To decorate
Chantilly Cream (see page 198)
Fresh fruits

Preheat the oven to 350°F (180°C). Grease and line two 7-inch (18 cm) round cake pans with parchment paper. In a large bowl, sift all the dry ingredients together. In a separate bowl, mix together all the wet ingredients and then add to the dry mixture. Mix until all the ingredients are well incorporated, but do not overmix.

Divide the batter between the pans and bake for 23 minutes until risen and firm to the touch. Cool in the pan for 10 minutes and then turn out onto a wire rack to cool completely. Decorate with Chantilly Cream and fresh fruits.

Cake will keep for 1–2 days in the refrigerator, stored in an airtight container. Allow to come up to room temperature before serving.

20 min. / 35 min.

Eggless, dairy-free, gluten-free, and with natural sweeteners, this cake has it all, including amazing moisture, flavor, and texture provided by the puréed carrots. Altogether a gorgeous carrot cake.

Carrot cake with yogurt frosting

Serves: 10

¾ cup plus 1 tablespoon (200 ml) sunflower oil, plus extra for greasing

1 cup (160 g) rice flour

¾ cup (115 g) cornstarch

1 cup (130 g) arrowroot

2 tablespoons baking powder

2 teaspoons ground cinnamon

1 teaspoon ground nutmeg

2 tablespoons flaxseeds

½ cup (100 g) coconut sugar

3½ tablespoons (50 ml) maple syrup

⅔ cup (150 g) Apple Purée (see page 164)

Zest and juice of 1 orange

8 oz. (225 g) cooked carrots, cooled and puréed

4 oz. (115 g) grated carrots

¾ cup (100 g) walnuts, chopped

Yogurt frosting

1 cup (250 g) coconut yogurt

1 tablespoon (25 g) honey

½ teaspoon vanilla extract

1 tablespoon lemon juice

Preheat the oven to 350°F (180°C). Grease and line a 9-inch (23 cm) springform cake pan with parchment paper. Sift the flour, cornstarch, arrowroot, baking powder, and spices together in a bowl. In a small bowl, mix the flaxseeds with ¼ cup (60 ml) water and leave to rest for 5 minutes to thicken. Mix the flaxseed mixture, sugar, maple syrup, apple purée, oil, and orange zest and juice. Add the carrots, mix well, and then add to the dry ingredients together with the walnuts. Mix until well combined.

Spoon the batter into the pan and bake for 35 minutes or until a skewer inserted in the center comes out clean. Cool the cake in the pan for 10 minutes and then carefully turn out onto a wire rack and leave to cool completely. Mix the yogurt frosting ingredients together in a bowl and then smooth over the top before serving.

Cake will keep for 1–2 days in the refrigerator, stored in an airtight container. Allow to come up to room temperature before serving.

dairy-, gluten-, and egg-free

10 min. / 45 min.

This is a really easy recipe for an eggless marble cake that is super soft, rich, and moist; the two distinct colors are mixed together in a marble effect.

Marble loaf cake

Serves: 8–10

½ cup (120 ml) sunflower oil, plus extra for greasing

1 cup (160 g) rice flour

½ cup (75 g) cornstarch

½ cup (65 g) arrowroot

1 teaspoon baking soda

½ teaspoon salt

7 tablespoons (150 g) honey

1 cup (250 g) coconut yogurt

2 teaspoons vanilla extract

1½ tablespoons apple cider vinegar

2 tablespoons raw cacao powder, sifted

Grated zest and juice of 1 orange

Preheat the oven to 350°F (180°C). Grease and line an 8 by 4-inch (800 ml) loaf pan with parchment paper. Sift the flour, cornstarch, and arrowroot with the baking soda and salt. In a bowl, whisk all the wet ingredients together and then mix with the dry ingredients until smooth. Divide the batter into 2 bowls and add the cacao to one and the orange juice and zest to the other and mix until combined.

Pour the 2 batters alternately into the pan and gently stir the batters with a skewer to get the marble effect. Bake for 45 minutes or until a skewer inserted in the center comes out clean. Leave to cool in the pan for 5 minutes and then turn out onto a wire rack to cool completely.

Cake will keep for 2–4 days in the refrigerator, stored in an airtight container. Allow to come up to room temperature before serving.

10 min. / 25 min.

This citrusy cake is packed with blueberries and makes a lovely cake for afternoon tea. It's not too sweet or tangy, but just right, and you could vary the flavors and swap for raspberries if you like.

Blueberry and lemon cake

Serves: 10

⅓ cup (80 ml) coconut oil, plus extra for greasing

¾ cup (120 g) rice flour

½ cup (65 g) cornstarch

½ cup (65 g) arrowroot

¼ teaspoon salt

2 teaspoons baking powder

½ teaspoon baking soda

½ teaspoon xanthan gum

1 tablespoon apple cider vinegar

½ cup (120 ml) almond milk

½ cup (100 g) coconut sugar

3½ tablespoons (50 ml) maple syrup

Grated zest of 1 lemon

2 teaspoons vanilla extract

5 oz. (150 g) blueberries

1 tablespoon powdered sugar, for dusting

Preheat the oven to 350°F (170°C). Grease and line a 9-inch (23 cm) square cake pan with parchment paper. Sift the flour, cornstarch, arrowroot, salt, baking powder, baking soda, and xanthan gum. Combine the vinegar with the milk and let sit for 15 minutes to make the buttermilk. Mix the sugar, syrup, oil, buttermilk, lemon zest, vanilla, and 2 tablespoons water in a bowl and then gently combine with the dry ingredients. Fold in the blueberries. Do not overmix.

Pour the batter into the pan and bake for 25 minutes or until a skewer inserted in the center comes out clean. Remove from the pan and leave to cool on a wire rack. Dust with powdered sugar.

Cake will keep for 2–4 days in the refrigerator, stored in an airtight container. Allow to come up to room temperature before serving.

dairy-, gluten-, and egg-free

5 min. / 18 min.

These cupcakes are soft, spongy, moist, and ridiculously chocolatey. They are made with apple cider vinegar, which gives you the best fluffy soft end product when combined with the leavening agent.

Chocolate cupcakes

Makes: 12

1 cup (120 g) sorghum flour
¾ cup (120 g) rice flour
⅓ cup (65 g) potato starch
½ cup (65 g) arrowroot
1¼ cups (250 g) coconut sugar
2 teaspoons baking soda
⅔ cup (50 g) raw cacao powder
1 teaspoon salt
2 tablespoons apple cider vinegar
Seeds from 1 vanilla bean (see page 21)
¾ cup (180 ml) sunflower oil
1½ recipes Chocolate Cashew Nut Frosting (see page 202)

Preheat the oven to 350°F (180°C). Line a 12-cup cupcake pan with cupcake liners. In a bowl, sift all the dry ingredients together and make a well in the center. In another bowl, mix the wet ingredients together with 1 cup (250 ml) water. Pour the wet ingredients into the dry ingredients and mix until thoroughly combined.

Pour the batter into the paper liners and bake for 18 minutes. Leave to cool in the pan for 10 minutes before turning out onto a wire rack to cool completely. Pipe the Chocolate Cashew Nut Frosting on top before serving.

Cupcakes will keep for 2–4 days in the refrigerator, stored in an airtight container. Allow to come up to room temperature before serving.

15 min. / 17 min.

These mini Bundt cakes are topped with a generous drizzle of lemon glaze, adding more moisture and lemon flavor. If you do not have a mini Bundt pan, you could make them as cupcakes.

Lemon and poppy seed mini Bundt cakes

Makes: 8
6 tablespoons (90 ml) coconut oil, melted, plus extra for greasing
½ cup (80 g) rice flour
⅓ cup (45 g) cornstarch
⅓ cup (45 g) arrowroot
2 teaspoons baking powder
½ teaspoon xanthan gum
½ teaspoon salt
¼ cup (50 g) coconut sugar
Grated zest of 3 lemons
1 tablespoon poppy seeds

2 tablespoons flaxseeds
3½ tablespoons (50 ml) maple syrup
Juice of 1 lemon
¼ cup (60 ml) oat milk
1 tablespoon chopped pistachios, to decorate

Lemon glaze
3 tablespoons powdered sugar
Juice of ½ lemon

Preheat the oven to 350°F (170°C). Grease an 8-cup mini Bundt pan. Mix the flour, cornstarch, arrowroot, baking powder, xanthan gum, salt, sugar, zest, and poppy seeds together in a large bowl. Combine the flaxseeds with 6 tablespoons (89 ml) water in another bowl and let sit for 5 minutes. In another bowl, combine the maple syrup, lemon juice, oil, and milk and whisk thoroughly. Add the flaxseeds and whisk. Pour the wet mix over the dry and fold to incorporate, but do not overmix.

Pour the batter into the pan and bake for 17 minutes or until a skewer inserted in the center comes out clean. Leave to cool slightly in the pan, then turn out onto a wire rack to cool completely. Mix the glaze ingredients together, then drizzle over the cakes once cooled and sprinkle with pistachios.

Cakes will keep for 2–4 days in the refrigerator, stored in an airtight container. Allow to come up to room temperature before serving.

5 min. / 50 min.

This deliciously sweet, easy to make, moist banana bread is made using very ripe bananas and studded with chocolate chips for an extra treat. The best cake for breakfast or snack.

Banana and chocolate chip loaf cake

Serves: 8–10

7 tablespoons (100 ml) sunflower oil, plus extra for greasing
¾ cup (120 g) rice flour
⅓ cup (60 g) cornstarch
½ cup (65 g) arrowroot
2 teaspoons baking powder
1 teaspoon baking soda
½ teaspoon xanthan gum
3 ripe bananas, mashed
2 tablespoons honey
3 tablespoons (40 g) coconut sugar
¾ cup (200 ml) rice milk
Seeds from 1 vanilla bean (see page 21)
½ cup (100 g) milk-free chocolate chips

Preheat the oven to 350°F (180°C). Grease and line an 8 by 4-inch (800 ml) loaf pan with parchment paper. Sift all the dry ingredients together in a bowl. Mix together the banana, honey, sugar, milk, oil, and vanilla seeds and then add them to the flour mixture and mix until just combined. Fold in the chocolate chips.

Transfer the batter to the pan and bake for 50 minutes or until a skewer inserted in the center comes out clean. Cover loosely with foil if it starts to brown too much. Cool in the pan for 5 minutes and then transfer to a wire rack to cool completely.

Cake will keep for 2–4 days in the refrigerator, stored in an airtight container. Allow to come up to room temperature before serving.

30 min. / 30 min.

The tangy, sweet pineapples in this cake work wonderfully well with honey. It is great served with a dollop of Greek yogurt.

Pineapple upside-down cake

Serves: 10–12

2½ cups (450 g) sliced pineapple, cored and thinly sliced lengthwise

4 teaspoons honey, plus extra for brushing

½ cup plus 1 tablespoon (125 g) unsalted butter, softened, plus extra for greasing

3 tablespoons flaxseeds

1 cup (100 g) spelt flour

½ cup (60 g) sorghum flour

⅓ cup (50 g) rice flour

¼ cup (40 g) potato starch

⅓ cup (45 g) arrowroot

1½ teaspoons baking powder

½ teaspoon baking soda

½ teaspoon xanthan gum

¾ cup (150 g) coconut sugar

½ cup (50 g) almond flour

1 cup (250 ml) buttermilk

Preheat the oven to 350°F (170°C). Place the pineapple, honey, and 1 cup (250 ml) water in a saucepan over medium heat. Bring to a boil and cook for 15 minutes. Remove the pineapple and set aside.

Grease and line an 8-inch (22 cm) round cake pan with parchment paper. Mix the flaxseeds with 6 tablespoons (89 ml) water and leave to rest for 5 minutes to thicken. Layer the pineapple over the base of the pan and pour over half the syrup. Sift the spelt, sorghum, and rice flour with the potato starch, arrowroot, baking powder, baking soda, and xanthan gum. Whisk the butter and sugar until smooth. Add the flaxseed mixture and stir to combine. Add the dry ingredients, almond flour, and buttermilk. Beat on low speed until just combined. Spoon the batter over the pineapple and smooth the top.

Bake for 30 minutes or until cooked and a skewer inserted in the center comes out clean. Cover loosely with foil if it starts to brown too much and bake with a baking tray underneath to catch any syrup drips. Leave to cool in the pan for 1 minute and then carefully turn out onto a serving plate. Brush with honey before serving.

Cake will keep for 2–4 days in the refrigerator, stored in an airtight container. Allow to come up to room temperature before serving.

10 min. / 60 min.

This easy, egg-free, moist honey cake will fill your house with a wonderfully sweet scent. Delicious as an afternoon treat with a cup of coffee or tea.

Honey and cinnamon loaf

Serves: 8–10

Vegetable oil, for greasing
½ cup (65 g) sorghum flour
½ cup (80 g) rice flour
¼ cup (40 g) potato starch
⅓ cup (45 g) arrowroot
1 teaspoon baking powder
1½ teaspoons baking soda
2 teaspoons ground cinnamon

½ cup (113 g) butter
⅓ cup (60 g) coconut sugar
½ cup (180 g) honey, plus extra for drizzling
Grated zest and juice of 2 oranges
⅔ cup (150 g) plain yogurt
3 bananas, mashed
Maple Glazed Pear Slices (see page 214), to decorate

Preheat the oven to 350°F (170°C). Grease and line an 8 by 4-inch (800 ml) loaf pan with parchment paper. In a bowl, sift all the dry ingredients together. Cream the butter and sugar until light and fluffy. Add all the other ingredients, except the bananas, and whisk until smooth. Fold in the mashed bananas.

Pour the batter into the pan and bake for 1 hour. Cool slightly in the pan and then turn out onto a wire rack to cool completely. Drizzle with honey and decorate with the dried pear slices.

Cake will keep for 2–4 days in the refrigerator, stored in an airtight container. Allow to come up to room temperature before serving.

dairy-, gluten-, and egg-free

10 min. / 30 min.

This is the perfect birthday or celebration cake and it is really simple to make. Soft chocolate sponge with avocado chocolate mousse and topped with fresh raspberries: It is a real showstopper cake to impress.

Chocolate and raspberry layer cake

Serves: 10
vegetable oil, for greasing
1 cup (160 g) rice flour
½ cup (85 g) cornstarch
⅔ cup (90 g) arrowroot
1½ teaspoons baking soda
⅔ cup (50 g) raw cacao powder
¼ teaspoon salt
½ teaspoon xanthan gum
1½ cups (250 g) coconut sugar
½ cup (120 ml) coconut oil
1¼ tablespoons apple cider vinegar
Seeds from 1 vanilla bean (see page 21)

To decorate
1½ recipes Chocolate Mousse (see page 210)
9 oz. (250 g) raspberries

Preheat the oven to 350°F (180°C). Grease and line two 8-inch (20 cm) round cake pans with parchment paper. In a bowl, sift together all the dry ingredients. In another bowl, mix the wet ingredients together with 2 cups (500 ml) water, add to the flour mixture, and stir until combined. Divide the batter between the pans and bake for 30 minutes or until risen and firm to the touch. Leave to cool in the pans for 5 minutes and then turn onto a wire rack to cool completely.

Sandwich the cakes together with half the Chocolate Mousse and raspberries. Spread the other half of the mousse on top and sides and top with the remaining raspberries.

Cake will keep for 1–2 days in the refrigerator, stored in an airtight container. Allow to come up to room temperature before serving.

NATURAL CAKE DECORATING

natural frostings

The rich fat content of cashews, almonds, and hazelnuts, mostly heart-healthy fats, makes them a perfect substitute for heavy cream and great for making frostings and spreads. In addition they are an excellent source of several vitamins, minerals, proteins, zinc, and antioxidants.

fresh fruit toppings

Fruit can be simple enough for everyday or elegant enough for special occasions—berries or sliced fruits arranged in an eye-catching pattern, frosted fruits with their vivid colors, or oven-baked citrus slices all make striking appearances.

egg-free mousses

Fruits like avocados and mangos with their fresh pulp can replace eggs in many desserts. They are as tasty as the traditional mousses, but they are practically fat-free, high in omega-3, heart-friendly, and contain little sugar.

dairy alternatives

Plant-based dairy alternatives will surprise you with their light, delicate flavor when using them as replacements for cream. Coconut milk can be whipped into a light cream to make mousses, cheesecakes, and frostings. Or swap heavy cream for light cream to lower the fat content in a recipe.

low-sugar sauces

Sauces and glazes add a sweet finishing touch. A simple glaze is usually made with refined powdered sugar and milk, but by using super nutrient-rich cashew nuts instead, you will create a real healthy treat.

natural jams

Fruit jams or coulis are a great way to add sweetness to a cake instead of using refined sugar. You can experiment with all kinds of fruit according to your personal taste—it is a great way to use overripe fruits. Jams are best used in combination with other fillings, such as a cream or chocolate sauce.

dairy-, gluten-, and egg-free

5 min. / 0 min.

This light whipped cream is a perfect side to most cakes but goes particularly well with Coconut and Rose Water Cake (see page 50), Carrot Cupcakes (see page 74), and Red Velvet Cupcakes (see page 84).

Whipped coconut cream

Makes: 14 oz. (400 g)

13.5-ounce (400 ml) can coconut milk

½ teaspoon vanilla extract

1 teaspoon honey

Keep the can of coconut milk in the fridge overnight. Scrape off the solid coconut fat and place in a food processor or blender together with the remaining ingredients. Whisk for 3–5 minutes until light and fluffy and then use immediately.

Keep in an airtight container in the fridge for 5 days.

gluten- and egg-free

15 min. / 2 min.

Chantilly cream

Makes: 1lb. (450 g)

3½ teaspoons agar

1⅔ cups (400 ml) heavy cream

2 tablespoons powdered sugar

2 teaspoons vanilla extract

Pour 2 tablespoons plus 1 teaspoon (35 ml) water into a small bowl and sprinkle in the agar. Leave to soften for 5 minutes. Transfer to a heatproof bowl set over a pan of simmering water (making sure the bottom of the bowl doesn't touch the water) and stir until the agar has dissolved. Whip the cream in a stand mixer for a few minutes before adding the sugar, agar, and vanilla. Chill for 1 hour and then whisk again before using.

Keep in an airtight container in the fridge for 2 days.

PREP / COOK TIME

5 min. / 10 min.

dairy-, gluten-, and egg-free

This recipe works well with fresh or frozen berries and is a great way to use up overripe berries. You could swap for any other berry.

Raspberry coulis

Makes: 10½ oz. (300 g)

10½ oz. (300 g) raspberries
2 tablespoons honey
Juice of ½ lemon
2 teaspoons vanilla extract

Place all the ingredients in a saucepan over medium-low heat. Mash the raspberries gently with a fork and allow the coulis to simmer and the honey to dissolve for about 10 minutes. Sieve the coulis if you don't want to see the seeds.

Keep in an airtight container in the fridge for 3 days.

dairy-, gluten-, and egg-free

10 min. / 0 min.

Cashew nuts are such a useful ingredient, as they can be turned into a creamy, rich, and naturally sweetened cashew cream. You can use it plain or on cakes, such as Chocolate Buckwheat Cupcakes (see page 182).

Cashew nut frosting

Makes: 13½ oz. (380 g)

1⅓ cups (200 g) cashew nuts, soaked for 4 hours and drained

½ cup (100 ml) coconut milk

1 teaspoon vanilla extract

½ tablespoon honey

Blend the cashews and half the milk in a food processor or blender for 2 minutes to a thick paste, stopping and scraping down the sides if needed. Slowly add the remaining milk and blend for another 2 minutes until smooth. Blend in the vanilla and honey.

For chocolate frosting: Add 1 oz. (25 g) raw cacao powder.
For coffee frosting: Dissolve 1 tablespoon instant coffee granules in 1 tablespoon boiling water and add to the frosting above.
For zesty frosting: Add 3 tablespoons lemon juice and 1 tablespoon grated lime zest.

Keep in an airtight container in the fridge for 5 days.

5 min. / 10 min.

These simple pan-fried banana slices are caramelized with coconut sugar, coconut oil, and vanilla extract for a simple and delicious treat. This recipe also works for other fruit, such as plums or apples.

Caramelized bananas

Makes: 20 slices

2 bananas, sliced

2 teaspoons coconut sugar

2 tablespoons coconut oil

½ teaspoon vanilla extract

Preheat the oven to 250°F (120°C). Dust the banana with coconut sugar. Heat half the oil in a skillet over medium heat and add some of the banana slices, spacing them out so they are not touching. Drizzle over half the vanilla extract. Cook for 5 minutes, or until caramelized on each side. Transfer the caramelized bananas to the oven on a baking tray to keep warm while you continue cooking the remaining bananas.

Keep in an airtight container in the fridge for 2 days.

20 min. / 0 min.

This spread goes well on hot toast over a layer of crunchy almond butter, eaten straight out of the jar with a spoon, or spread on a cake like Chocolate Avocado Cake (see page 98).

Hazelnut and chocolate spread

Makes: 12 oz. (350 g)

1⅔ cups (250 g) raw hazelnuts, roughly chopped

3 tablespoons (45 ml) maple syrup

5 tablespoons (75 ml) sunflower oil

3 tablespoons (45 ml) almond milk

3 tablespoons (20 g) raw cacao powder

Seeds from 1 vanilla bean (see page 21)

Pinch of salt

Preheat the oven to 350°F (170°C). Place the hazelnuts on a baking tray and roast for 12–15 minutes. Leave to cool slightly before removing the skins. Place the hazelnuts in a food processor or blender and blitz until they turn into a paste, scraping down the sides as needed. Add the syrup, oil, and milk in small batches and mix well. Add the cacao, vanilla, and salt and blend well until creamy and smooth.

Keep in the fridge for up to 3 days or freeze. If frozen, leave out to defrost and stir before using.

15 min. / 35 min.

You can experiment with different ratios and types of berries in this jam, depending on your preference and what's ripe at the time.

Mixed berry and vanilla jam

Makes: 1lb. 2 oz. (500 g)

14 oz. (400 g) mixed blackberries, raspberries, and blueberries
Seeds from 1 vanilla bean (see page 21)
½ cup (100 g) Apple Purée (see page 164)
2 tablespoons honey
Juice of ½ lemon

Place all the ingredients in a saucepan over low heat. Bring to a boil, stirring, and cook for 35 minutes. Leave to cool and settle for 10–15 minutes before ladling into a sterilized jar and sealing.

The jam will keep unopened for 1 year but, once opened, store for up to 3 months in the fridge.

dairy-, gluten-, and egg-free

5 min. / 0 min.

This mousse is a super-easy dessert. It can also be frozen in an ice cube tray; when you're ready to eat it, either defrost it or throw the cubes straight into a blender and enjoy half frozen.

Avocado and chocolate mousse

Makes: 12 oz. (340 g)

2 ripe avocados (240 g), peeled and pitted

Pinch of salt

6 Medjool dates, pitted

5 teaspoons coconut sugar

1 teaspoon vanilla extract

⅓ cup (90 ml) almond milk

2 tablespoons coconut oil

⅔ cup (60 g) raw cacao powder

Place the avocados, salt, and dates in a food processor or blender and blend until smooth. Add the sugar with the vanilla, milk, oil, and cacao powder and blend again until completely combined, scraping down the sides occasionally. Taste and add more sugar, if necessary.

Keep in an airtight container in the fridge for 3 days.

5 min. / 5 min.

This creamy, eggless mango curd is quick and easy to make and a perfect way to use up fresh mangoes. Ready in less than 10 minutes, it goes well spread on toast or pancakes, or swirled into yogurt or ice cream.

Mango curd

Makes: 14 oz. (400 g)

1 tablespoon arrowroot powder
1 tablespoon (15 ml) lemon juice
12 oz. (335 g) mango, diced
1½ tablespoons (25 ml) maple syrup
2 tablespoons (30 ml) coconut milk
Pulp from 2 passion fruit

In a small bowl, combine the arrowroot powder with 3 tablespoons (45 ml) water and the lemon juice, and stir to combine. Purée half the mango in a food processor or blender until smooth and then place in a small saucepan and cook until bubbling, stirring constantly. Add the maple syrup and then the arrowroot mixture and cook for another 2 minutes. Remove from the heat and add the milk, remaining mango, and passion fruit pulp. Leave to cool before using.

The curd can be stored in a sterilized sealed jar in the fridge for up to 3 days.

dairy-, gluten-, and egg-free

5 min. / 3 hours

These glazed citrus slices are perfect as decorations around the home and will also make your home smell incredible. This recipe also works well for other type of fruits like apple and pear.

Maple glazed citrus slices

Makes: 30 slices

1 lemon, sliced

1 orange, sliced

2 teaspoons maple syrup

Preheat the oven to 200°F (100°C). Line a baking tray with parchment paper. Arrange the fruit slices on the tray, without overlapping, and brush with the maple syrup. Bake for 3 hours, or until the peels have dried and the flesh has turned translucent.

Once cooled and dried you can use immediately or store in an airtight container in the fridge for a week or in the freezer for 3 months.

dairy-, gluten-, and egg-free

15 min. / 0 min.

This creamy icing is a healthy version of
a traditional cream cheese icing. You could also
make a colored version by adding 1 teaspoon
almond milk and 2 teaspoons of your favorite fruit
powder (see page 11).

Creamy cashew icing

**Makes: 3½ oz.
(100 g)**
3 tablespoons (50 g)
cashew nut butter
2 tablespoons coconut
milk
2 tablespoons coconut oil
1 tablespoon honey
1 teaspoon vanilla
extract

Place all the ingredients in a bowl and whisk just to combine,
scraping down the sides as you mix.

Keep in an airtight container in the fridge for 5 days.

10 min. / 0 min.

Smooth, spreadable, and creamy, this recipe proves that you don't need butter to make a fudgy chocolate frosting, plus, it's easier to make.

Fudge frosting

Makes: 1lb. 2 oz. (500 g)

1 cup (150 g) cashews, soaked for 4 hours and drained

1¼ cups (175 g) Medjool dates, pitted

¼ teaspoon salt

½ cup (40 g) raw cacao powder

Seeds from 1 vanilla bean (see page 21)

⅓ cup (80 ml) coconut oil

Place the cashew nuts, dates, and salt in a food processor or blender and blend until smooth. Add the cacao powder, vanilla, and oil and blend again until smooth, creamy, and thick, scraping down the sides occasionally.

Keep in an airtight container in the fridge for 3 days.

dairy-, gluten-, and egg-free

5 min. / 0 min.

A healthy chocolate sauce using organic, unrefined coconut oil, raw cacao powder, and maple syrup. Unlike the store-bought one, this sauce has vitamins and antioxidants because of the raw cacao.

Cacao sauce

Makes: 9 oz. (250 g)

¼ cup (60 ml) coconut oil, melted

½ cup (120 ml) maple syrup

⅔ cup (50 g) raw cacao powder

1 teaspoon vanilla extract

Place the coconut oil, maple syrup, cacao powder, and vanilla in a food processor or blender and blitz until combined. Add 2 tablespoons water slowly and blitz again until smooth.

Use immediately or set aside in the fridge for 10 minutes to thicken.

index

acknowledgements

I would like to say a huge thank you to my publisher, Catie Ziller; you always inspire me to give my best. To my amazing photographer, Lisa Linder, for being the best partner in this journey and for making my cakes look beautiful. A big thank you goes to Abi Waters and Michelle Tilly for their editorial work and great design. To my husband Salvatore and my children Luca, Andrea, and Mario.

First published in 2019 by Hachette Livre (Marabout).

This edition published in 2024 by Hardie Grant North America, an imprint of Hardie Grant Publishing.

Hardie Grant

NORTH AMERICA

Hardie Grant North America

2912 Telegraph Ave
Berkeley, CA 94705

hardiegrantusa.com

ISBN 9781958417539
ISBN 9781958417546 (eBook)

Library of congress cataloging-in-publication data is available upon request.

Copyright text © 2019 by Marabout

For the Marabout edition:

Publisher: Catie Ziller
Photographer: Lisa Linder
Editor: Abi Waters
Designer: Michelle Tilly

FSC MIX Paper | Supporting responsible forestry FSC™ C020056
www.fsc.org